"*In Hold That Thought*, Gem Fadling's voice is both bright and grounding, able to meet readers where we are and also kind enough not to leave us there for long. Through her own stories and the stories of others, Gem submits a helpful and accessible guide to discerning between the competing internal voices we all contend with, always circling back to the wisdom of our true voice and the present nearness of God."

Emily P. Freeman, author of *The Next Right Thing*

"*Hold That Thought* is a gem of a book that intertwines teachable moments through everyday personalities who seek God's directives on their spiritual journeys. Within these personal stories, Gem integrates a theological foundation and personal testimonies that encourage readers to live a transformative life steeped in embracing God's agape love. From such a foundation, individuals are empowered to take control of their voices and speak God's truth over their life; they are equipped to experience inner healing, godly success, and freedom in Christ. This is a must-read for those seeking to drink deeper!"

Barbara L. Peacock, author of *Soul Care in African American Practice* and founder of Barbara L. Peacock Ministries

"I often hear people ask who the desert fathers and mothers, the abbas and ammas, are today. While they are few and far between, I am delighted to suggest Gem Fadling is one. As a spiritual mother, she guides readers skillfully and deeply into the inner landscape of the soul. *Hold That Thought* is the kind of resource I wish I'd had for myself twenty years ago. So, I adjure you: Be brave. Open these pages and confront your inner voices of shame, pain, and isolation. They will begin as enemies but end as friends on the holy journey toward wholeness."

Tara M. Owens, spiritual director and executive director of Anam Cara Ministries, author of *Embracing the Body*

"Desires and longing are the lifeblood of a vital, joyous, and dynamic life, a life worth living. For too long desires and longing never hit my agenda, and burnout was the result. Gem writes in *Hold That Thought*, 'We must get in touch with our truest longings and our deepest desires. These are God-given and are the key to becoming more authentically us, inwardly and outwardly.' Spirit uses desires and longing as an invitation for living our most expansive and heart-centered lives. The unsettled heart cannot afford to be ignored; it offers us the keys to the kingdom life where the heart arouses us in wonder, curiosity, and ultimately, freedom."

Juanita C. Rasmus, spiritual director and author of *Learning to Be*

"You've heard the voices that make you believe that if you want to get anywhere in life, you need to hustle more and push harder. This book helps you identify those debilitating voices and untangle them from your heart and mind. Gem Fadling is a wise and trustworthy guide for any of us who have listened too long to the inner voices that make us strive and try harder. Read this book and find your own true voice in the process."

Jennifer Dukes Lee, author of *Growing Slow* and *It's All Under Control*

"Starting from her own prayer for needed change, Gem Fadling takes on the voices of achievement, control, and angst to show us where these voices come from and then how to participate in God's life. Gracious, generous, and practical, *Hold That Thought* walks us through discernment with God so we can live the abundant life Jesus promises. If you're feeling stuck, or transformation feels too opaque, *Hold That Thought* is a kind companion."

Ashley Hales, author of *A Spacious Life* and *Finding Holy in the Suburbs*

"If you are ready to understand why you think the way you do and want godly, practical ways to shift unhelpful thoughts, this is the book for you. Gem Fadling normalizes the common human struggle through sharing from her personal story and the stories of others. She gives permission to address the deep thoughts in our minds that are not helpful. The questions throughout the pages will help reshape the thoughts that are no longer serving you well. As a pastor, I will be recommending this book to a lot of people. It is worth picking up and journeying through no matter where you find yourself in life's journey."

Diana Shiflett, pastor and author of *Spiritual Practices in Community*

"*Hold That Thought* is a wonderfully practical guide to move from self-contempt into curiosity and compassion. Gem Fadling is both relatable and refreshing—a wise and kind voice who will help you better hear the Voice of Love in your life. *Hold That Thought* is theologically rich, accessible, and psychologically astute. I'm so grateful to have this book as a resource for my clients and community!"

K.J. Ramsey, licensed professional counselor and author of *The Lord Is My Courage*

Hold That Thought

Sorting Through the Voices in Our Heads

Gem Fadling

An imprint of InterVarsity Press
Downers Grove, Illinois

InterVarsity Press
P.O. Box 1400 | Downers Grove, IL 60515-1426
ivpress.com | email@ivpress.com

InterVarsity Press® is the publishing division of InterVarsity Christian Fellowship/USA®. For more information, visit intervarsity.org.

All Scripture quotations, unless otherwise indicated, are taken from The Holy Bible, New International Version®, NIV®. Copyright © 1973, 1978, 1984, 2011 by Biblica, Inc.™ Used by permission of Zondervan. All rights reserved worldwide. www.zondervan.com. The "NIV" and "New International Version" are trademarks registered in the United States Patent and Trademark Office by Biblica, Inc.™

While any stories in this book are true, some names and identifying information may have been changed to protect the privacy of individuals.

The publisher cannot verify the accuracy or functionality of website URLs used in this book beyond the date of publication.

Cover design and image composite: David Fassett
Interior design: Jeanna Wiggins

ISBN 978-0-8308-3169-2 (print) | ISBN 978-0-8308-4696-2 (digital)

Printed in the United States of America ∞

Library of Congress Cataloging-in-Publication Data
A catalog record for this book is available from the Library of Congress.

29 28 27 26 25 24 23 22 | 8 7 6 5 4 3 2 1

FOR ALAN

These two hearts . . . never apart.

*Between stimulus and response there is a space.
In that space lies our power to choose. And in
our choice lies our growth and our freedom.*

ATTRIBUTED TO VIKTOR FRANKL

*Be transformed by the
renewing of your mind.*

ROMANS 12:2

Contents

You Are More Than Your Thoughts

"IT SOUNDS TO ME LIKE YOU HAD AN ANXIETY ATTACK."

"What? I can't experience an anxiety attack. I run an organization called Unhurried Living. This is really off brand," I thought to myself, tongue in cheek. "How did this happen?"

Here's the thing . . . I already knew what triggered it. I just couldn't get it to stop.

TRIGGERS AND MY THOUGHT LIFE

A few years prior, we had launched our own non-profit, Unhurried Living. It had been a wonderful experience and yet the same dynamics that make it amazing, also make it stressful—building something from scratch, discerning how best to serve, creating continuous inspirational content, training, teaching, and travel. I love every part of what I do. But as we were building our organization, I experienced recurring run-ins with my newfound ambition and an anxious straining. These bouts of anxiety would build up and about once a year, I would hit a wall. I would continue to work but inside, the car was running out of gas and the type of fuel changed without notice. My body would speak up (usually through exhaustion), and I would make necessary adjustments in my thinking and in the *way* I was working.

To be clear, I was, in fact, drinking my own unhurried Kool-Aid: I was practicing the things we teach people through Unhurried Living and had done so for years. And yet there was still something about the way I was (or wasn't) managing my anxiety and stress that began to take a toll. The fourth yearly occurrence of this pressure ended up being more than I could handle with my regular patterns. Looking back, I now see that the unaddressed voices of the Stressed Achiever and the Inner Critic were wreaking havoc.

At the time, we were talking with a consultant about a new program we were going to launch along with the marketing efforts surrounding it. Before I knew it, this conversation triggered[1] me, and I descended into a spiral of anxiety. We were rolling along just fine until the consultant mentioned the timeline: the new program would begin in just one month. In his mind, the timing made sense because we would be riding the wake of another offering. But hearing that date sent shock waves through my body.

You're not ready.

You'll never keep up.

What are you thinking? You can't do this.

There isn't enough time.

What if it doesn't work?

These were just some of the thoughts that comingled with my adrenaline and sent me into fight or flight mode. This became the handle that turned on the flow of anxiety. These thoughts flooded in like a raging river, I accepted them as my own, and I became overwhelmed at the idea of beginning a new aspect of our work. Undiscerned thoughts will often do this. Rather than leaving our thoughts unexamined, it is better to engage the Inner Observer, that aspect of ourselves that can step back from the subjectivity of the moment.[2] The Inner Observer is a non-biased aspect that can help us, along with the Holy Spirit, to take time to notice, discern, and respond. I had become acquainted with my Inner Observer many years before but, for some reason, she took the day off, and I was swept away by the roaring rapids of anxiety.

Even with my regular spiritual practices, I was unable to manage the level of stress I was feeling. I continued to push, and, at the same time, I didn't pause to process the anxiety in my emotions or my body. Unconscious drives kept the spigot turned on. So, I called my former counselor for a checkup.

I would find out later from my counselor that I was experiencing the pulsating release of adrenaline, and thankfully he helped me learn how to manage this dynamic. Normally, once adrenaline is released, it washes through. However, I felt the heightened sensations in my body and then added lots of unhelpful thoughts that culminated in ongoing, anxiety-producing aftershocks. For a few weeks, I was on high alert all day, every day. I began to feel like the sole of a worn-out shoe; I was moving forward, but I had no traction.

In addition, I knew I would need a refreshed re-working of my thoughts as they sent me into the ongoing, unrelenting, pulsing waves of anxiety. I was being invited to dig down even deeper into the well to find new levels of some much-needed freedom.

> I began to feel like the sole of a worn-out shoe; I was moving forward, but I had no traction.

A REFRESHED FOUNDATION

A Tuscan vacation had long been a dream of mine. I'd seen the romantic movies and the Rick Steves documentaries of rolling hillsides and views for miles. I thought it would be the perfect way to celebrate our thirty-fourth wedding anniversary. We had not been on a real vacation for a few years, the kind that was dreamed of, planned for, and set aside as a sacred unplugging. Many of our recent vacations consisted of a few days added on to work trips, so we were way overdue for this kind of rest and replenishment.

Because of my husband, Alan's, international travels for the previous few years, we had saved up a nice stock of miles. So, I began my research by talking to friends who had been to Italy and re-engaged Rick's videos to get the lay of the land. After carefully choosing, editing, and pruning our list, we came up with the perfect trip. The bulk of the two weeks would be spent in Tuscany, with a little Barcelona, Spain, added onto the end of the trip for good measure.

With my anxiety attack just a couple of months prior, I was intent on our getaway being more like a pilgrimage than a vacation. I entered our European anniversary trip with a single prayer: *God, you have to show me a new way to live and work. My current way is no longer serving me, and I need a new level of sustainability and peace.*

For our first full day in Florence, we made a reservation to climb to the top of the Duomo in the Cathedral. Four hundred and sixty-three steps to the top with multiple dark, concrete, spiral staircases going up, up, up. The climb to the top of the Duomo was long and arduous, sometimes feeling claustrophobic. Jet lag had left me without much stamina, and much of the time I was winded. There was one distinct moment when I didn't know if I could keep going as the walls pressed in tightly around me. *Was it going to get more closed in? Could I hang in there all the way to the top?* This was evidently the price you pay for a staggering view and perspective—literally and metaphorically.

With quad muscles quaking, I finally made it to the top of the Florence Cathedral. Relieved, I began my quiet stroll around the three-hundred-sixty–degree dome, pausing here and there to look out over the city. I found myself searching for exhilaration. I was trying to feel something. Anything. Some sparkly sensation of *I'm doing something amazing right now!* But as I searched within, all I sensed was flat numbness where I expected excitement to be. Experiencing part jet lag, part exertion from the stair climb, and part exhaustion from the previous months of anxiety, I stared out over the rooftops.

Slowly, and invited by the Spirit, my search for excitement turned into a prayer of gratitude. I moved from anticipation to contentment through gratitude in the moment. I enjoyed the softness, the quietness, of this inner shift, and I whispered, "Thank you." I took a deep breath as a soft smile emerged.

After climbing the Duomo, I took time to wander the Cathedral. I sat down in the side chapel that contained the bread for Eucharist. Behind the ciborium (the container designed to hold the eucharistic bread), there was a large painting of *The Last Supper*. For the first time in a long while, I finally felt like myself. Just me. Sitting. Being.

As I stared at the ciborium, in my mind I heard the phrase I hear every week during Eucharist: *This is my body, given for you.* It was followed by this pointed invitation: *Stop pushing. Stop trying. Stop angsting.*

These were the perfect words for my situation and the spiritual counsel I so desperately needed. I willingly received this message. This unholy trio was exactly what I experienced, and it no longer served me in any way. The time on that pew was quite relaxing and peaceful. My heart and mind were now open to God anew. My prayer for a new way was already being answered.

YOU ARE NOT YOUR THOUGHTS

You are not your thoughts. The first time I heard this wisdom from the desert fathers and mothers, I was stumped. These are my words, my commentary, and my voice. Of course, my thoughts are me. But even though I barely understood what it meant at the time, something about this insight rang true. Another way to say this in the positive is, *you are more than your thoughts.* As I began to take in this reality, a huge sheet of glacial ice slid from the mountain of my understanding about what goes on inside my own head.

At the onset of a triggering event, I easily move into a series of thoughts. The Anxious Controller joins in chorus with the Inner Critic, and these thoughts (which we will identify synonymously as "voices") lead to unhelpful emotions. Before I know it, I'm on an unwilled slide into pushing, trying, or angsting. But I am not my thoughts; that voice I hear is not necessarily my truest self; and I do, in fact, have a choice about my response.

Of course, by now, many of us have a rudimentary understanding of what is occurring in our brains because of the developments in the field of neuroscience. We have learned, with great delight, that we can change our brains. Neuroplasticity shows the patterns that have formed can be renewed. We no longer believe in being stuck. We can pick up the needle and move it into a new groove, one that we create with new thoughts! Sounds simple, but it is far from easy. It takes a great amount of courage and effort to become open to change, aware of your thoughts, and willing to do something about them.

Romans 12:2 says, "Be transformed by the renewing of your mind." This is a beautiful invitation to engage thought work. And yet it is in the passive: "Be transformed." We are reminded to cooperate with God's work of making all things new within us. Engagement with this transforming process is much more fruitful than heeding the advice of the Positive Thinker, who isn't always grounded in reality, or the Passive Spectator, who prefers to play it safe. I needed to engage a new way of thinking so I wouldn't fall prey to stress the same way in the future. I carried my prayer for help all the way to Italy, and God met me there.

PUSHING, TRYING, AND ANGSTING

I was invited to stop pushing, trying, and angsting. But what does this mean? How do these dynamics show up in my life, and why are they so unhelpful? Let's take a look at these particular dynamics that heightened my anxiety and were named by the Spirit in the Florence Cathedral.

Stop pushing. Pushing is what we do when we want to have a sense of control. We know that controlling others and circumstances is an illusion and yet we still try. We aren't happy to let the ball roll down the hill and so we find ways to move against it, pushing it upward by sheer might. This is exhausting and, if left unchecked, is a straight line toward meltdowns or burnout. I had succumbed to pushing when I unconsciously gave way to the false belief that *I am what I do.*[3] The multi-faceted nature of my work easily led to overwhelm. This caused me to search for ways to control my environment. And when on a quest for control, perfectionism slides easily into place. Perfectionism is a terrible master because it demands 110 percent, and it has no tolerance for subpar work. You can see how pushing emerges as a natural result of this. I . . . must . . . do . . . more . . . to . . . be . . . more. These unhelpful thoughts emerge when pushing: *You've got to manage this. You can't let anything slide. You've got to defend yourself or this will leave your control. Keep doing something!* Even if you don't consciously see these thoughts, you can usually feel them in your body and the need to push grows stronger.

The desire for power and control[4] that leads to pushing shows up in Thomas Keating's programs for happiness (power/control, affection/esteem, and security/safety). There is nothing wrong with them and these instincts are necessary for human development. They are built in so humans can survive and thrive. And yet, as we continue to make our way forward, we'll see that many of our unhelpful thoughts find their genesis in our search for fulfilling one or more of these unconscious drives in an unhealthy way.

Pushing occurs when the desire for power and control goes unchecked. But when I pause and remember that *I already have what I need*, I realize I need not *do* more to *be* more, and I don't have to keep pushing that ball up the hill. I can relax into the situation and pushing can take a rest.

Stop trying. Trying is what we do when we want to have a sense of value. As my identity became more wrapped up in my work, I often looked outward for affirmation. This type of trying is like rowing a boat to an unknown and likely unreachable destination. It is unreachable because the affirmation monster is never fully satisfied. How much more encouragement do you need to stay afloat? Just a little more. The thoughts that came up for me were: *What* *will people think? What if I look or sound stupid? I need a large following to validate what I'm doing. I can't offend anyone. What if people don't like me?*

Trying is what emerges when I give in to the unconscious belief that *I am what others say about me.*[5] I continue rowing to receive other people's approval, accolades, and affirmation instead of rowing for pleasure or out of my giftedness. The kind of exhaustion this causes is more emotional and mental than physical. It comes from the deep desire for esteem and affection.[6] Aiming to please others is another unruly taskmaster because it leaves you at the whim of other people's behavior and expectations. You end up being on the end of other people's chains and if they don't rattle them just the way you want, it can lead to more distress. And so, you continue to try.

As I pause and remember that *I already have what I need,* I can lay down the oars and begin to float on the ocean of God's love. I remember I am already loved exactly as I am, and the drive to try diminishes.

Stop angsting. Angsting is what emerges when we want to have a sense of safety. When we don't feel safe, anxiety and worry combine to create a sense of angst. The thing about angst is that it is unfocused, and it manifests like a generalized blanket of dread. It hovers so that you don't really notice it or name it, you just feel the weight of it. It's like carrying around a heavy, wet woolen blanket draped over your shoulders. This was the sensation I began to feel as my anxieties revved up. Thoughts like these would float by and overwhelm me: *This is too much. You can't keep up with this. What have you gotten yourself into?* Undiscerned, these thoughts lead to a foreboding sense that something horrible could occur at any moment.

Angsting is a search for security and safety[7] and the false identity of *I am what I have.*[8] I believe it is the stuff around me—whether material, relational, or emotional—that will keep me safe. For some, this creates a surrounding flurry as they seek more and more stimuli to keep these voices at bay. Others, and maybe most of us, turn to numbing. Angsting can be an overwhelming sensation so sometimes we suppress the anxious feelings and move toward whatever takes the pain away. The easy ones are substances, food, and media. But numbing can occur in any number of possible ways, including diving into unhealthy relationships or mindless shopping. The list could go on. In fact, numbing occurs when we are doing anything to escape our actual life, our reality.

When I pause and remember that *I already have what I need* I can finally take off that dense wet blanket of angst and relax into the love of God. I begin to experience Jesus as the Prince of Peace, and I realize I can learn to cope with my life with greater ease.

YOU ALREADY HAVE WHAT YOU NEED

After a couple of days in Florence, we drove to Assisi. Having no idea what was in store for us, Assisi would quickly become one of our new favorite locations. As in Florence, we took time to meander the Basilica of Saint Francis. By this time, we were a few days into our vacation, and I easily walked at a strolling pace. I wandered one of the enclaves of the basilica, still carrying with me a prayer for a refreshed way to live and work. As I moved through the large space, in my heart I sensed the Holy Spirit saying: *You already have what you need. You may have lost track of it. You may have forgotten it. But you have it. Life is a journey of uncovering.*

Our vision of God matters a great deal here. God is not a distant, stoic entity whose location is out beyond the reach of the Hubble

Space Telescope. We are not trying to pull God close so that he can see and hear us. We are not banging on a locked door trying to get God interested in what we are doing. Cognitively, we would all likely agree that this is the case. And yet we don't always *feel* it is true. I held onto this image for a long time. God was some distant old man that I would have to coerce to come my way. I wouldn't have said this out loud because it was more of an underlying feeling than a conscious thought.

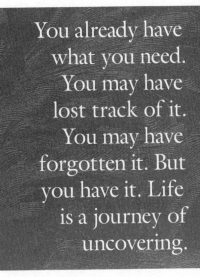

You already have what you need. You may have lost track of it. You may have forgotten it. But you have it. Life is a journey of uncovering.

When we talk about the love of God, it is more like you are sinking into something—or rather someone—who is already right there. In *The Divine Conspiracy*, Dallas Willard wrote, "But do we actually believe this? I mean, are we ready automatically to act as if we stand here and now and always in the presence of the great being . . . who fills and overflows all space, including the atmosphere around our body?"[9] This description was a major shift for me, and I came to refer to this idea as, *God is not elsewhere*. It's another way of saying, "God is near" but the twist of "not elsewhere" shines a light on my former belief and turns it on its head. When I say this out loud, it helps me to remember that God is right here, the very air I am breathing. This is the heartbeat of Acts 17:28, "In him we live and move and have our being."

Contemplative practitioner and clinical psychologist Dr. James Finley, on his *Turning to the Mystics* podcast, said it like this:

And if love is the fullness of presence, then just one thing is happening, this love is pouring itself out and giving itself away, see, that we are the song that God sings. And this is so radical that if God were to cease loving us into the present moment, at the count of three, we'd disappear, because we are nothing, absolutely nothing, apart from the love of God.[10]

God is not elsewhere. Becoming more settled into this reality is the key to everything. You are not alone. No matter what you are going through. God is present and you are being held together by love. This is at the heart of my Assisi insight: *You already have what you need.*

Pushing, trying, and angsting are red lights on the dashboard that remind me to pause and check in with myself. As I engage a self-check, I can begin to embrace the idea that I already have what I need, I can open my heart more fully to love. It is love that sustains me inwardly, so I won't be owned by Nouwen's false identities or Keating's programs for happiness. Even a brief pause can give you some space to re-orient yourself to the truth. You can learn to breathe into the situation, allowing the dynamics of pushing, trying, or angsting to relax.

You will find that 2 Corinthians 13:14 contains a blessing that speaks directly to our desire to be embraced by the Trinity: "May the grace of the Lord Jesus Christ, and the love of God, and the fellowship of the Holy Spirit be with you all." The Trinity lives in a perfect union of love. As much as we are invited to notice our thoughts, we are also graciously being wooed into the trinitarian embrace. This is the heartbeat of *you already have what you need.* And just outside that inner circle lies this truth: "His divine power has granted to us everything pertaining to life and godliness, through the true knowledge of Him who called us by His own glory and excellence" (2 Peter 1:3 NASB).

It is the love of God, the grace of Jesus, and the fellowship of the Holy Spirit that empowers us from within. If we stay in our heads by focusing only on our thoughts and narratives, our inner work may soon become hollow and lifeless. The organic engine that generates lasting change is the undercurrent of trinitarian love. This means everything you *need* access to, you *have* access to. This requires receptivity and an acceptance of process. There may be

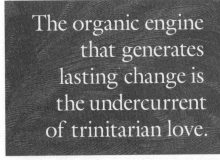

The organic engine that generates lasting change is the undercurrent of trinitarian love.

layers on top of layers that require uncovering before we can experience the fullness of this verse. But the pursuit is part of it. Let's look at the love of the Father, Son, and Spirit as we continue to be more open, aware, and willing to receive their love.

The love of God. In Matthew 3:16-17 we find that as Jesus was being baptized, a voice was heard from heaven: "This is my son, whom I love; with him I am well pleased." Built into this sentence is unconditional love and acceptance.

In a spirit of prayer, let's personalize this sentence using the feminine, and feel free to read these words aloud: "This is my daughter, whom I love; with her I am well pleased." How does that feel?

Now, slightly more personal, I'll use my name (feel free to insert your own): "This is Gem, whom I love; with her I am well pleased."

Finally, hear God saying this to you in the first person: "Gem, I love you; you are so pleasing to me."

When I find myself pushing, I can pause to hear God call me his daughter. *You are my daughter.* This sense of family care can calm my need to manage and control. When I'm trying, I can hear God speak of his love for me. *Whom I love.* This love can quell my need to look everywhere else for esteem or value. When I'm angsting, I can hear God's affirmation. *With you I am well pleased.* This love can relax my anxious heart, and I remember I am always perfectly safe in the kingdom of God.

The grace of Jesus. Each Sunday in my Anglican church as the bread is held up before me, the priest utters these beautiful words: "This is the body of Christ, given for you." It is this phrase that Jesus offered to me in the Florence Cathedral: *This is my body, given for you.* Each word speaks beautifully of love and swims in grace. When I'm pushing, I can remember that Jesus *gave* his very life, his body, for me. When I am trying, I can remember that Jesus gave *himself* willingly, a gift. When I am angsting, I can remember that Jesus gave himself *for me.* My body. Given. For you.

The fellowship of the Spirit. In the upper room, Jesus reminded the disciples that he and the Father would not abandon them but would leave a helper, the Spirit. "I will ask the Father, and he will give you another advocate to help you and be with you forever—the Spirit of truth" (John 14:16-17). Jesus continues in verse 26: "the Advocate, the Holy Spirit, whom the Father will send in my name, will teach you all things and will remind you of everything I have said to you."

When I'm pushing, I can remember that the Spirit promises to teach and *remind me* of everything Jesus has said. When I'm trying, I can remember that the Spirit will indeed *help me.* I am not alone. Ever. When I'm angsting, I can remember that the Spirit will *be with me* forever. Embracing eternity can surely talk me off the ledge of my anxieties.

The love of the Father. The grace of Jesus. The fellowship of the Holy Spirit. Trinitarian love is the foundation on which we build our thought work. And we can work on both concurrently. We don't have to put anything off. We simply take our next step on the path of love as well as the highway of our thoughts.

PERSONIFICATION OF VOICES

In the animated Disney movie *Inside Out*, emotions such as joy, sadness, and anger were personified so we could look at them objectively. We were invited to hear from them and learn about ourselves and others. In a similar way, I'd like to personify some of the voices we have in our heads so that we can detach a bit and see them from a distance. In this way, we may be able to engage our Inner Observer and gain a little more insight into the monologues, dialogues, and diatribes that float through our brains on any given day.

There are some voices that do not simply drift through; they are more deeply ingrained. So much so that we make the mistake of thinking that the voices and thoughts are, in fact, us. But, as we were reminded from classic spirituality, we are not our thoughts, we *have* thoughts. These inner voices are thoughts, and we can learn to notice, discern, and respond to them. I have chosen a few common inner voices and have given them names so that we can take a more objective look at each one. We are influenced by these voices, and yet we have the power to befriend, integrate, and release much of the angst that comes from allowing them to take the driver's seat.

Each of these inner voices can become our teachers as we learn to listen to them. But we must remain in the driver's seat of our own lives. We decide which thoughts to focus on and what we do once we've noticed what is being said. This path toward maturity takes practice. We won't get it perfect, but we can make tremendous progress in our ability not to be taken captive by fearful or controlling inner voices. There is no need to judge any of these voices. This adds to their shame, and they devolve into the worst form of themselves as they go unseen, unheard, and unacknowledged. It is our acknowledgment of them that liberates us to experience a more full, rich, and free life. If we do not look the voices squarely in the eye, we might remain trapped in unhelpful and unhealthy ways.

At its core, each voice does not believe it already has what it needs. So, it finds a way to whisper (or yell) in your ear to get your attention. When faced with the truth *you already have what you need*, the voices may lash out:

No, you don't. You don't have enough control. What if things go awry? What will happen then, huh?!

No, you don't. You haven't achieved enough yet. You haven't proved yourself. Get on it!

No, you don't. You can't possibly have everything yet. But I know how to get it. Let's go!

No, you don't. It's not perfect yet. We are going to get this right if it's the last thing we do.

No, you don't. That other person is keeping you from being happy. If they would just change, then you'd have what you need. Until then you are stuck.

No, you don't. And you don't know how to get it. You only have so much energy and we've got more important things to do like hide, be scared, and remain unfulfilled. That way you never have to be disappointed.

No, you don't. How could you possibly fill that giant void in your heart? There is no way to fill up this space, and even if you try there's no way it will happen any time soon.

Seeing the voices this starkly can make us either laugh or cry. But when these unhelpful thoughts circle around in our brain, they seem very real—and they feel like the truth. After I chose these seven voices and began to unpack them, I realized many of them have managing tendencies found in internal family systems (IFS).[11] It makes sense that these energies would emerge because pushing, trying, and angsting easily leads to a manager-type dynamic. IFS refers to our different "parts" that arise to help us along the way. These parts rise up over the course of our lives—including traumatic experiences—and they do help us cope. However, each part may become increasingly unhelpful as they keep us stuck in patterns that no longer serve us. Ideally, we can learn to befriend these parts and let them know that our adult, maturing self can take it from here.

As a reminder, I am not coming at this from a therapeutic frame because I am not a therapist. I am coming alongside you as a spiritual director and a soul care coach. We'll take a look at a handful of ways we try to manage ourselves, our relationships, and our responsibilities. These voices may appear to us as thoughts, feelings, or intuitions. They are not an exhaustive list of every dynamic or inner voice. They are a handful of ways we can grow in awareness of our various parts. Together, we can learn to identify these seven voices and any others that arise. And we can notice, discern, and respond our way to greater wholeness.

In the next chapter, we'll look at making necessary choices, engaging our whole self, and choosing fruitful action. I'll also introduce an important practice—Notice, Discern, and Respond—as we take a deep dive into each of the seven voices. Thank you for investing in yourself by being willing to engage your own thoughts as well as God's love. I pray you'll find the freedom you are looking for.

REFLECTION QUESTIONS

- ◉ In what area(s) of your life do you notice a tendency for pushing, trying, or angsting?
- ◉ What does it mean to you that *God is not elsewhere*?
- ◉ How aware are you of your own Inner Observer? How might you engage your Inner Observer more often?
- ◉ With which unbelief objection did you resonate most?

Finding Your Voice

2

IN THE MOVIE *WONDER WOMAN*, Diana has been raised and trained as a warrior. Steve, a young World War I pilot, crashes on her remote island, and she resolves to go with him to help with the raging war.[1] After making their way past a few obstacles, they arrive at No Man's Land. The two opposing sides have been at a stalemate for almost a year. No one has taken any ground. Steve and the men engage with the guys in the bunker, and a heated conversation between Steve and Diana ensues.

Steve assures Diana nothing can be done. He persists by saying it is impossible to cross No Man's Land. Diana is perplexed and cannot believe what she is hearing. She is determined to act, so she turns her back as she unfurls her updo hair. In slow motion, she turns around, and we see her in her Wonder Woman crown and garb, as a new emboldened version of herself emerges.

As she climbs out of the bunker, our view flashes on her shield, arm bands, boots, and golden lasso. For the first time, she *chooses* to be herself, in all her fullness. She emerges into the burned landscape and gray sky of No Man's Land. Bombs explode all around as she strides boldly into the space between the warring factions. In slow motion, a lone bullet is shot from the other side. As it makes its way to her, she waves her cuffed arm, and it ricochets away. The scene cuts to her face as we glimpse a tiny smirk and a determined twinkle in her eye. She gains more strength and courage to continue her journey across No Man's Land. The music swells as bullet after bullet is deflected. Steve and his men gain the courage to follow her as they all emerge from the bunker. In the middle of the field, she is hit with a melee of machine gun bullets as the camera pans an overhead view. She takes *all* the hits with her shield. This gives Steve and his men an advantage, and they manage to overtake the men in the opposing bunker.

> She simply needed to act on what was within her.

No Man's Land is the location of Diana's awakening. The truth is, she already had what she needed. She had trained as an Amazon warrior. Courage and fortitude simmered deep within. Her entire life journey led her to the center of that field.

She simply needed to act on what was within her.

She was alive to her voice, power, and choice, and she embraced and owned it. Along the way, all the moments of her life counted— the moments of training, of insight, of action, and, yes, of failure. The moment Diana steps out into No Man's Land is a major turning point. But this did not happen all by itself out of nowhere. Everything counted leading up to that moment.

A NECESSARY CHOICE

I remember watching an interview with Patty Jenkins, the director of the *Wonder Woman* movie. She mentioned that she had to fight to get the No Man's Land scene placed into the movie. Some thought it was unnecessary and slowed the movie down. But she knew instinctively that it was the inflection point of the movie and crucial to Diana's story. Jenkins was right. It was absolutely necessary to witness Diana choosing to become who she already was.

How ironic that a woman had to use her voice to fight for a scene in which a woman steps into her own voice. And how telling that others were sure this part of the story was unnecessary. Isn't it sometimes the same in our own lives? People all around suggesting what is and is not important for and to us.

Finding our voice and stepping into who we are is a beautiful part of our own personal story. This movement is critical—especially for the second half of life. Whatever we build in the first half gets to play out beautifully, lyrically, cinematically in the second half as we continue to shed the false self and step into who we are. No one's life is perfect. We all still have struggles, fears, and self-doubt. However, we can enjoy a new sense of wisdom, grace, and focus. And these dynamics are beautiful to experience and witness.

Wonder Woman's No Man's Land graphically represents our own thought landscape. Unhelpful thoughts fire at us, seeking to derail or keep us stuck. But like Diana's golden cuffs, we have the power to stop the unhelpful thought in its track by noticing, discerning, and responding. As we move past each "thought-bullet" our confidence grows, causing our freedom to increase and our voice to emerge.

MY VOICE BEFORE

During the first half of my life, I would describe myself as not having my voice. This means I couldn't always identify what I wanted or what I needed. And even when I did, I didn't speak up for myself. This wasn't true 100 percent of the time, of course. I was still a functioning adult who could hold down a job, manage a household, and raise children. But there was this huge piece missing . . . what I'm calling here *my God-given voice.* As I began to wake up to this more and more, three dynamics of my non-voice rose to the surface.

I apologized for taking up space. Many years ago, I was teaching at a leadership retreat. We recorded our talks so we could put them online for the participants to refer to later, and I was the one who edited and uploaded the talks online. One time, as I was listening to a recording of myself, I realized I was talking way too fast. Some of that might have been nerves, but I do remember feeling as though I needed to hurry up so that (1) whoever was next could get up there and (2) I could get out of people's way. My fast talking was a kind of apologizing for myself. *I'm sorry I'm here, taking up this space. I'll finish up real quick so the important things can happen.* This was an undercurrent I began to notice in myself in these kinds of situations. I wasn't believing in and standing in my own value, and I wasn't speaking from a holy confidence in what God had placed inside of me.

There may be any number of undercurrents running under the surface of our lives. It is good to be aware of this dynamic so that we aren't held back unnecessarily. An undercurrent can feel like a low hum of a thought that you usually don't hear unless you take time to listen. Sometimes these thoughts can be brought to the surface as we unpack a difficult or frustrating situation with a friend or even a time of journaling. We can learn to listen more deeply to ourselves on our formational journey.

I rarely said "I." When I talked about any version of my life history, I always said "we." The "we" was Alan (my husband) and me. Part of the reason for this is that I met Alan when I was seventeen, began dating when I was nineteen, and got married when I was twenty-one. We grew up together in every sense and were tied at the hip in life and ministry from our earliest days. I was basically groomed for this because, in my mother's mind, the most important part of being a woman was to be married and have children. So, this became an early goal for me. However, this forced ideal, paired with the dysfunction we both brought into our marriage from our families of origin, was a setup for classic enmeshment.

This was solidified by the conservative church culture at the time that encouraged the duties of the "pastor's wife" and women in general. Intentional or not, trying to fit into a role as a Christian woman can lead to various versions of unhealth and even spiritual trauma. Many of us have some unlearning and major healing to engage in this regard. It is okay to have a healthy sense of self and not just be known in relation to someone else. I, as an individual, am one whom God dearly loves and it's okay to believe, embrace, and live this.

My husband and I enjoyed partnership in ministry and most of my stories did include both of us. This is a great strength in our lives even to this day. But I didn't have a clear sense of "just me." I didn't have a resounding "I." This showed up clearly during my time in counseling. We had become enmeshed, and part of our work was to become independent. Our counselor worked diligently to move us from dependent to independent to interdependent. It turns out that interdependence is much more enjoyable. It allows both people to be who they are and to connect and contribute to the marriage in a healthier way.

After all the difficult inner healing work was done and I was graduating from and debriefing my process with my counselor, he let me in on a little secret. When we began, my self-esteem was so

low and my use of the word "we" was so prevalent that he wasn't
sure he was going to find *me*. I'm embarrassed as I share this. I had
no idea I was so un-present in my own life. With his help, the
skillful guidance of the Holy Spirit, and my concerted engagement,
I did, in fact, find *me*. And the beautiful energy of that continues
to increase.

I couldn't say, "I deserve." I realize that the idea of deserving
may get sticky here for some. Many of us have been taught that we
don't deserve anything. Why else would you need grace, mercy, or
forgiveness? But my self-esteem took a hit in a way that didn't lead
to received grace. It led to an undervaluing and even a devaluing of
myself. Grace is supposed to be a loving, inspiring, inviting part of
the story, and it is—but somehow my self-worth got trampled down
in the midst. My relationship to "I don't deserve" was unhealthy,
and I wasn't in touch with my inherent value and worth as a child
of God and as a human being. The focus of the word "deserve"
wasn't so much on the demand within it, but on my lack of healthy
esteem for myself as a holy and beloved daughter.

I couldn't say yes to any phrase that contained the word "deserve." Not even, *Do you deserve to be loved?* I understand that "deserve" can be a loaded word. But if you don't think you deserve
anything, that is too low a view of yourself and that is not what
God intends. When God created humans, he said we were "very
good." A healthy level of worthiness, rooted in Genesis 1, was
needed in my case simply to bring me up to a base level. Let's re-
claim the idea of being worthy. I am worthy of love. I am worthy
of respect. And Jesus underscored our worth and value by giving
his very life for us all.

In the current season of my life, these three dynamics are no
longer the boss of me. I am more confident than I have ever been. I

don't apologize for taking up space. I know how to say "I." And I have a healthier connection to the idea of being worthy. Does this mean I never have low self-esteem or that I never struggle with self-doubt? Of course not. But I am not held back or controlled by those moments. My baseline is more confident and assured. I am indeed a beloved child of God, lovingly created and cared for. My gifts and calling are sure. And I am more often living in that flow.

Coming to terms with these dynamics is important not only for my own self-esteem and confidence. It is also critical for my relationship with God and others. For a long-term love relationship with God, a too low view of myself may keep me from receiving all God has for me and extending that same grace to others. God's view of us is at the center of our life, relationships, and work. If I apologize for taking up space, if I don't have a healthy sense of "I," and if I believe I don't deserve anything, how am I to embrace the love of God at ever deepening levels? God's love, care, and desire to know me are measureless and unending. How can I be as open as possible to continually receive this love? Just as interdependence works well in a marriage, it also works in our relationship with God. I don't have to think too high or too low of myself. I can see myself rightly through the eyes of God who lovingly created me and is transforming me, over time, into the image of Christ. I can then call out that same goodness in the lives of others and in a spirit that is conducive to the message.

> God's love, care, and desire to know me are measureless and unending. How can I be as open as possible to continually receive this love?

HOLISTIC TRANSFORMATION

As much as this book is about our thoughts, we must also include our hearts and our bodies. Our thoughts, feelings, and actions all work together in one harmonious composition. We might focus on only one aspect at a time, but that doesn't mean they are separate from one another. Thoughts are a nice place to begin because all of us have multiple thoughts throughout the day, and it's relatively easy to stop and notice what is going on inside our brains. However, the inner work we are describing here involves the whole self. Sometimes our body takes the lead by exhibiting exhaustion or illness. Other times, our emotions wave a warning flag to catch our attention. Sometimes, it's both. In fact, our brains take cues from our autonomic nervous system as it crafts stories to make sense of what is occurring around us.[2] We are focusing on the idea of thoughts and voices because this is *one* way we can intentionally cooperate with "be transformed." Don't think that because we are focusing on thoughts, we are negating or dismissing any other part of ourselves. We are complex beings, and all these dynamics are intertwined.

A couple of Scripture passages rise to the surface here as we consider this transformation process. In Colossians, Paul describes a life of fullness, freedom, and being alive. This invitation is ours as well:

> Since, then, you have been raised with Christ, set your hearts on things above, where Christ is, seated at the right hand of God. Set your minds on things above, not on earthly things. For you died, and your life is now hidden with Christ in God. When Christ, who is your life, appears, then you also will appear with him in glory. (Colossians 3:1-4)

In Philippians, Paul continues with encouragement to engage good, fruitful, and helpful thinking:

> Finally, brothers and sisters, whatever is true, whatever is noble, whatever is right, whatever is pure, whatever is lovely, whatever is admirable—if anything is excellent or praiseworthy—think about such things. (Philippians 4:8)

Rather than seeing these passages as another set of commands we aren't achieving, or to-do lists we never quite complete, they appear as wisdom and an invitation to a more loving way to live in the space between our ears. When I took my "I need another way to do this" prayer with me into the Italian cathedrals, it was my attempt to set my mind on things above. My real and present situation gave me the opportunity to reach for more helpful thoughts and ways of being. If I am, indeed, hidden with Christ in God, then my truest self is intact and accessible, which makes all of this *invitational* and *doable*, two of my favorite dynamics.

Why would God, who names himself "Love," continue to remind us over and over about the grace of Jesus, and the fellowship of the Holy Spirit, and then make living this life impossible? I choose to believe that what is written in these passages are not simply commands barked from a distant, heavenly megaphone, but the loving instruction of a wise counselor, a nurturing parent, and the shepherd of my heart.

True, noble, right, pure, lovely, admirable, excellent, and praiseworthy—this is not an insurmountably high bar we can never reach. These are invitations to choose a better way. Look at that list again. I bet you truly want to think about such things. The beauty is you can make the choice to do so. And there are two dynamics that help us here: love and self-control.

Living water of love. Many of our cultural issues stem from a basic need for people to be seen, known, and loved. Think about any aspect of culture you saw in the news in the last week. There are multiple issues within any given story; however, at the base of many issues are these dynamics: *I want you to see me. I want you to know me. I want you to accept me. I want you to love me.*

When we traveled to Israel many years ago, part of our tour included the Qumran caves. I was struck by the aqueduct system that carried fresh water off the mountain and into the living space of the people. In the case of the mikvah (the ritual bath that people went through before offering their sacrifices), the water moved into a cistern, where the silt floated to the bottom. The clean water flowed out an opening at the top of the cistern and made its way into the mikvah. The ritual bath could not contain "dead water." It had to maintain contact with a flowing, natural water source in order to be considered "living." Only moving, living water was considered holy and pure.

In like manner, how can we stay in connection with the living water of love? "Let anyone who is thirsty come to me and drink. Whoever believes in me, as Scripture has said, rivers of living water will flow from within them" (John 7:37-38). Jesus is, of course, referring to the Spirit here. And remember that the first fruit of the Spirit listed in 1 Corinthians 13 is *love. In him we live and move and have our being* reaches in yet again. Within this holy space, we have access to rivers of living water flowing freely from within us, the first fruits of which is love. You already have what you need. Love is within you, and you are capable of growing in your embrace and expression of this love.

Choosing the good. I have often heard (and taught) that none of us can control anything. And this is true. We cannot control situations or people. No matter how hard we try, everything is completely out of our control. But isn't it interesting that one of the fruits of the Spirit is "*self*-control"? As a fruit of the Spirit's work in our life, we actually do have control . . . of ourselves. We have the benefit of being able to make choices about what we think and what we do. Typically, we think of self-control in negative terms. It becomes the *oomph!* we use to keep ourselves in line while dieting or trying not to gossip. It's the energy we use to not do the things we are not supposed to do. But self-control is so much more than that . . . and it is about choosing and taking positive action.

I get to choose to think helpful thoughts.

I get to choose to speak uplifting words.

I get to choose to love and serve others.

Self-control is the gift of being able to choose what is good. Not merely *not* do what is bad. We have access to Spirit-given self-control. We get to choose what we focus on and how we respond. Since self-control is a fruit of the Spirit, that means we don't have to force it or pump it up from somewhere inside of us. Remembering that we already have what we need, we can let this self-control emerge more and more as we grow in our discerned responses. As we consider the voices in this book, we'll use our energies for good to make our way along the path of change.

As we move forward, I encourage you to engage the power of presence to stay in reality, here and now. This is how you notice what is actually occurring. It may not be easy at first, but addressing it in grace and truth, and facing it in the best possible sense, is a healthy way to live. In the present moment, we can be honest about our weaknesses or shortcomings. It is in the *now* that we find the strength for transformation. If you want to grow, the only place to begin is right where you are and as you are. You can start planting the seeds of change in the ground right in front of you. Most of us are aware of what is going on in the surface levels of our lives. However, our deepest places may still seem mysterious. There may be places of awareness that you have suppressed or denied or pushed aside because it's too difficult to admit. It may be too embarrassing, shaming, or fearful. When you are ready, these areas are the fertile ground for growth, the perfect place to participate in the gardening of your soul.

> If you want to grow, the only place to begin is right where you are and as you are. You can start planting the seeds of change in the ground right in front of you.

NOTICE, DISCERN, AND RESPOND

Notice, Discern, and Respond (NDR) is an empowering approach to working with your thoughts. It is a practice that my husband, Alan, initially titled "unhurrying your thoughts"[3] and one that we have shared with leaders around the world. I have greatly expanded on the idea of NDR and have been using this model in my coaching groups with women, and it has been bearing good fruit in that context as well.

Holocaust survivor and psychiatrist Victor Frankl is attributed with saying, "Between stimulus and response there is a space. In that space lies our power to choose. And in our choice lies our growth and our freedom."[4] I'm suggesting that NDR is one process you can engage in that space. Armed with the empowering NDR process, you can move a thought from unhelpful to helpful. You can lean into powerful and gracious questions so that your own inner Spirit-led wisdom can help you make your way forward. And the beauty is it works whether you are making a quick shift or if the change will take some time. Once you become familiar with this simple practice, it can become an underlying way of discerning as you engage your own thoughts. Let's take a look at moving through the process of NDR.

Notice. Take the time to notice an unhelpful thought. As you work with the thought, at first, simply see it. Write it down and look at it. You cannot change what you do not see. You don't have to judge the thought; you can simply notice and hold it in God's presence. Built into this kind of noticing is the beginning of acceptance. You are no longer hiding from the truth. Noticing leads to discernment and is especially helpful when working with desires or weaknesses.

Discern. Discerning is about becoming more curious. Openness and honesty really help here so that you can uncover what is really going on. Look at the unhelpful thought you noticed and wrote down. What is the tone? Is thinking this thought still working for you? Is it true? Will this be a quick shift, or will it take some time to change this pattern? In God's presence, turn these questions into prayers, and let yourself explore. Discernment isn't simply about finding answers. Holding the questions themselves can be stretching and deepening. Use helpful inner-process resources, engage with a wise friend or counselor, or empty your thoughts into your journal. Learn more about yourself and the issue. Discernment is the key to becoming wiser and more confident. It is also the precursor to more healthy responses. Some thoughts will shift easily and some with require more time. Either way, in time, you can move toward responding.

Respond. Once you have spent some time discerning your thought, what is one simple shift you can make or step you can take? Rather than reacting, you can move gently through Notice and Discern into Respond. Responding then becomes an overflow rather than a manufactured headlock you place on yourself. Action flows freely in response to what you've noticed and discerned. And remember that sometimes your action may not be an outward to do. It may be more about receptivity or some other dynamic of remaining open. Process matters in this case, especially if you want to make lasting change. In the work of changing your thought, consider a reframe and the shift you would like to make. This may happen quickly or, depending on how deeply this thought is anchored within, it may take a while. But either way, simply take the next step and keep going until you have a new healthy pattern.

At the end of each voice chapter, you will have a chance to engage NDR specific to that voice. A few questions are provided to guide you into the beginning of your exploration of each voice. Appendix B contains an extended NDR flow you can use as you work with one thought at a time. Engaging thought work by examining the voices that pop up can lead to greater freedom in your life with God and with others.

Notice that I use the words *helpful* and *unhelpful*. Not good and bad, or even positive and negative. The real question here is whether it's helpful or not. We don't need to judge our thoughts; we simply decide if they are helping us move toward wholeness and then adjust as necessary.

For example, anger, and the thoughts surrounding it, is usually considered bad or negative. But, at times, harnessing our anger can lead to healing or move us toward necessary action. We also tend to think sad thoughts are bad. But sadness helps us move through our grief. Both anger and sadness are inevitable on the way to the deepest healing. So be careful about how you label a thought or a feeling.

Good and *bad* are binary terms and we are so much more complicated than that. On the extreme ends of binary thinking, we may end up with either toxic positivity or nihilism. We are trying to address the healthy middle here, the daily struggle to not be trapped by our thoughts or emotions. To think and to feel are both good and necessary, and we want to learn how to live healthy versions of ourselves in the midst of the ups and downs. With discernment and proper companionship, you can walk this journey toward wholeness.

THE INNER DINING TABLE

When working with these seven voices, and any others you notice, it can be good to picture yourself at the head of a dining table.[5] You have the seat of honor, and you make all final decisions. In thought work, you can imagine these voices sitting around the table. They speak, but they don't have the final say. You can take the time to hear them, befriend them, and discern whether or not to move forward based on their suggestions.

As you engage the voices, you may notice they seem to have a hold on you at various levels. There are three levels you might notice right away.

First, some voices speak, and you can see quickly and clearly that what they are saying doesn't serve you any longer. So, you notice them and thank them for their help. Then you remind them that you can take it from here, and you come up with a new thought that works better for you, one that moves you forward in a healthy manner.

Second, some voices may speak, and you realize their ways are tied to some very old and unhealthy patterns in your life. You can see that it is going to take a while to undo that thought habit and begin a new one. But you know that with ongoing discernment and practice, you can carve a new mental pathway, and you choose to do so.

Third, overcoming some voices may require the help of a counselor, spiritual director, or coach. Some thoughts are so old and so deep that you need someone to walk alongside you as you make your way.

Of course, knowing the difference between levels two and three may take its own discernment. One reason I am more able to make my way on my own (level two) is because of the deep work of healing I encountered in my own counseling experience (level three). As I found healing from my past and learned to engage my own voice, my confidence and freedom grew. The more steps you take toward healing, the more freedom is available, and you begin to experience a snowball effect.

As for level three, here are a few signs you might need additional help:

If you are unable to carry out your day-to-day responsibilities.

If you find that your dynamics are tied to a past trauma.

If you feel stuck in a younger version of yourself.

If you keep trying, but you never seem to get a leg up.

If any voice feels like it has a stranglehold on you, it might be a sign that this has escalated to a point where it's time to seek help.

This will require further planning and even budgeting, but please know the investment is worth it. Many therapists and spiritual directors work on a sliding scale and that can help a great deal. A healthy you is one of the best gifts you can give to yourself and those around you. It's never too late to take care of yourself, and you can begin right where you are.

Well, it's time to dig into our seven voices. This is in no way an exhaustive list, but these are a good representation of the kinds of thoughts we have in common. My guess is you will recognize most of them. Some may come into play more than others; however, you have likely experienced each of them at one time or another. Every voice chapter contains a vignette from the life of a real woman as she made her way from one way of thinking to another. I want to thank these women who chose to share very personal aspects of their own journeys. I've used pseudonyms to protect their privacy, and I could not be more grateful for their vulnerability.

Together, let's be unafraid to look these voices squarely in the eye and admit how they may have led to pushing, trying, and angsting. And, at the same time, let's thank them for being pointers of the way to greater wholeness and strength.

REFLECTION QUESTIONS

- How might you borrow Wonder Woman's courage to step into your own No Man's Land as you engage your thoughts?
- Describe the "before" version of your own voice. Where do you find yourself in this process of becoming?
- What would it look like to engage Spirit-given self-control for positive movement forward?
- How might you ensure you remain at the head of your own inner dining table in relation to your thoughts?

3

From Stressed Achiever to Living with Intention

WITH A DARK AND OMINOUS SKY AS A BACKDROP, I found myself standing on the edge of a precipice. In silence, I peered over the dusty edge into the cloudy darkness below. A slight breeze lifted and swirled a few fallen dry maple leaves behind me. Amid the quiet, I heard a holy invitation: *Jump*. It was a leap of faith. I felt emotional, but not afraid. I knew, without a doubt, I would not hit the ground. Rather, I would be caught in the arms of the One who loves me without reservation. This was all about trust—leaping into the unknown of my future and believing what was out there was good—even though I couldn't see past the darkness.

This mini prayer-movie played out in my mind during a worship service at a Christian family camp. I was in my mid-thirties and our three sons were ages two, five, and eight. We were preparing to take a one-year sabbatical from ministry. I didn't know it at the time, but this sabbatical was part of my initiation into the midlife journey. I closed my eyes and surrendered afresh my life to God. It wasn't the first time I had surrendered, but it was a major turning point for me.

I had participated in various forms of church ministry for over fifteen years. Over the course of that time, I had worked with junior high schoolers, high schoolers, college students, young adults, women, and couples. I had served on women's ministry boards and had facilitated a MOPS—Mothers of Preschoolers—group. I had been on worship teams, prayer teams, and mission teams. And, in the early, pre-children years of our marriage, I participated in all of the college ministry activities while holding down a full-time job in the corporate world. It makes me tired just to think about it.

Back in my prayer-movie, before my leap of faith, I hesitated for just a moment. I looked back, because I knew it was time to say goodbye to the way things had been. I expected to see a large, glowing pile of achievements. Instead, I caught sight of a drab green tent and a small stack of cardboard packing boxes. "That's it?" I thought. "That's all there is? That's not so hard to leave behind." Inherently, I knew, even though I could not see clearly, what was waiting for me in the unknown was far greater.

So, I metaphorically jumped off my metaphorical trust-cliff and into the dark chasm of sabbatical and midlife.

The sabbatical year itself was a master class in simplicity and letting go. All of my outside markers, titles, and responsibilities were gone. There were no jobs that proved my identity. By the time I got to the end of that year, I had been boiled down to a single moniker: *Child of God. Hello,* I thought to myself, *I'm Gem Fadling, Child of God.* Everything was the same and yet everything had changed. I had been cut down to a single stalk and all the fruitful branches had been pruned.

As if that weren't enough, at the end of the sabbatical year another image emerged as an addendum to the cliff-jumping-tent-leaving season. I had made it to the other side of the valley that lay beneath the dark clouds of the faith jump. I had walked along the valley-floor-of-pruning and had reached a sheer cliff. It was pitch black with a lone spotlight that shone on me where I stood. Looming before me was a completely flat (no hand holds) mountain wall with a single rope hanging down from above. The invitation was simple: *Climb.* Over the next many years, I would engage an arduous process of further inner refinement. What's interesting to me now is how stark these two early invitations were: *Jump. Climb.* No descriptions. No map. Just simple trust.

Our sabbatical year was foundational to what came next. I wouldn't have been able to bear the years of inner work that followed without knowing, in my deepest self, that my truest identity was in God alone. This was the pillow that cushioned everything to come. My touchpoint. The invitations to jump and climb became the next deep dive into learning presence. I wasn't merely receiving instructions from God and then attending to them like a faithful servant. It was the deepening of the words in John 15: *Apart from me you can do nothing. I no longer call you servants. I call you friends.* This touches the deep heart cry of the voice of the Stressed Achiever. You are more than what you do. You are loved without question.

You are more than what you do. You are loved without question.

Anyone who is in or has moved through midlife knows it can be extraordinarily uncomfortable. Pruning, disorientation, wilderness experiences, tested faith, ruminating doubts, and deep regrets abound. However, it was sheer grace to be reminded up front that I was, at my center, a beloved child of God and a friend of Jesus.

THE VOICE OF THE STRESSED ACHIEVER

The voice of the Stressed Achiever lives loud and strong in the first half of life. It can also sneak in when you are building something new in any season of life, as I found out as we began building Unhurried Living. The Stressed Achiever is the voice that pushed me along the path toward my anxiety attack. *Staying busy proves my worth. The more I produce, the more I am. Someone must push this thing up the hill. Let's get going!*

It is easy to find yourself worried about your to-do list. There is much to do. The Stressed Achiever likes to focus on tasks, action items, and accomplishments. And, whether she wants to admit it or not, she usually cares very much what others think. She also likes to chastise you when you give yourself a break. She is never satisfied and abhors resting, which she equates with laziness. At her worst, she is the voice of the taskmaster, cracking the whip of pushing with the added battering rams of trying and angsting. The Stressed Achiever is relentless because underneath it all, she fears that she doesn't exist apart from her achievements. She is afraid that if the truth came out, she would discover that she is just a shell. She is also afraid that, without achievements, she might be unlikable or unlovable. This tends to be at the base of her driven-ness and why she spends so much time *doing*. At least this "proves" her existence, value, and worth.

The Stressed Achiever often lives under the weight of productivity. She has a constant and demanding to-do list that helps her to feel accomplished. She gets things done. No weeds grow under her feet. Tasks are being checked off left and right, and her worth and value are tied to accomplishing the list. The trap here is that the list can never, ever be completed. It simply grows longer. If there is no list, and nothing to achieve, how will I exist? It is easy to see how stress moves in and takes hold.

The Stressed Achiever is likely the voice that moves you to sit at the front of the class and drives you to make friends with the teacher rather than the students. She wants you to excel, and perfectionism easily slips into the mix. Once perfectionism moves in, the weight of this voice can become unbearable. What will it take to quell the relentless pushing of the Stressed Achiever?

The Stressed Achiever must come to terms with being loved apart from accomplishments. There is nothing wrong with a to-do list. It's good to get things done, but it's not helpful to tie our value to it. The search for value gets buried underneath the swirl of the productivity we feel compelled to engage. The list is fine—it keeps us organized—but it is not the most important aspect. Knowing I'm loved is central because it moves me to *become*. And becoming is crucial to our accomplishing. This is the beautiful idea of overflow—living from the inside out. Who I am informs what I do and breathes life into how I show up in the world.

> Who I am informs what I do and breathes life into how I show up in the world.

ISABELLA'S STRESSED ACHIEVER

Isabella[1] had been a strong worker her entire life. Growing up, if she wasn't busy with school, she was dancing. She was always capable, always busy, and always achieving. So, in her mid-twenties, as she stepped into her first career in the tech field, her familiar patterns kicked into high gear. She was either running at 100 mph or 0 mph—nothing in between. So much so that she found herself frequently ill due to lack of rest. Overworked and on the verge of burnout, Isabella began to dream of a different life—that of an entrepreneur. She wanted to set her own hours and be her own boss, so she left the tech industry and began to work full time for herself. However, she often found herself working in front of her computer for eight hours straight with no breaks as she became obsessive and addicted to work. She quickly found out the pacing of her life wasn't as externally driven as she thought. The pushing was inside of her and had followed her from the tech field into her home office.

A common thought when she was in the tech business was, *When I leave here, then I can live the way I want.* Did the thoughts change when she became an entrepreneur? No. She was still thinking the same thoughts: *When my business reaches this milestone, then I can live the way I want. Then I will rest more.* She always had a future vision for rest, not a present vision for it. Underneath, a low hum began to emerge: *When am I going to get to that place where I give myself permission to enjoy my life?*

Dissatisfied with this cycle, Isabella began the journey of looking within. There was nothing wrong with Isabella's midwestern upbringing. Working hard is good and so is pouring yourself fully into your work. But, somehow, amid these good roots began to grow weeds that choked out her peace and joy. She discovered a few unhelpful thoughts among the weeds. These thoughts were driving her further and further from the inner pacing she so longed for.

I'm only making money when I'm doing.

If I slow down, I will lose everything.

I will feel okay once I get everything checked off my to-do list.

Once I get there, all will be good.

These thoughts led to actions that worked for her . . . until they didn't. *There has to be another way!* became her heart's cry. Soon, God intervened as only God can. At just the right time, mentors and coaches entered Isabella's life and began to hold space for her to explore her true values, motivations, and intentions. She began to share her longings for a different way, even though she didn't know how to make the necessary changes. She discovered that it was near to impossible to make deep, lasting change on her own. She said yes to support as her mentors shone a light into her life, reminding her of her desires and supporting her as she moved forward.

Isabella's big discovery? Patience. She could grow and change as she was able. She didn't have to push to get ahead. She didn't have to be on call 24-7. Her value was not based on her accomplishments but rather on being the beloved daughter of a caring God. This informed her very being and she began to live and work out of that place. Like a sculptor, God chipped away at what was unnecessary, and Isabella cooperated with the process. Over time, she began to see the beautiful sculpture at the center of the block of marble . . . her truest self, already seen, known, and loved. Is it a wonder that a different kind of work emerges from such a woman?

New thoughts and beliefs began to emerge:

My worth is not tied to my doing.

My to-do list will not make me feel safe.

The more I take care of myself, the more my business grows.

The Spirit is my business partner.

You can see in these new thoughts that Isabella had transitioned from outward achievement to inward care and stability. And she began to see the connection between her inner self and her work. Lasting peace and contentment were elusive before she made this shift. She's still growing and learning, but she more readily makes her way to choices that are life-giving and in alignment with her desires and intentions. Her quality of work and even the quality of her marriage improved. Relationships and work improve when *we* grow. Opportunities now flow toward Isabella in the form of speaking engagements, clients, and more. She will be the first to tell you that she more consistently makes space for rest, play, and fun—and that she feels more in flow now than ever before. Is everything perfect? No. But the Stressed Achiever has taken the back seat, and Isabella is more often enjoying the ride of her life.

MOVE FROM A+ TO B+

The Stressed Achiever typically feels the need to be at the top of the class. She needs the attaboy of an A+. But what if you could make the small shift of being willing to put out B+ work? It's likely that some of you are breaking out into hives as you read this. *What?! What is this B+ you speak of? I can't allow that to happen. Do you know how that reflects on me?* And there she is, tipping her hand. The Stressed Achiever cares deeply about how she will be perceived.

Let's look at this for a moment. If the Stressed Achiever has been doing her job so far, you probably have very high standards, and the level of your work is likely above and beyond what most others could accomplish. So, practically speaking, your B+ work is probably an A for most other people. What could be the harm in relaxing a bit, by allowing the Stressed Achiever to rise up and then subside? You could choose to believe that you are fully capable of putting out high quality work without pushing, trying, or angsting. You could relax into the reality that you are, indeed, a loved and valued person of quality and that what you produce is already very good. As you begin to believe this more and more, then the Stressed Achiever doesn't have to rise up so often to push you along.

INTENTION AND DIRECTION

As we begin to move away from the clamor for an A+, we can shift our attention to a new way forward. When it comes to matters of the soul, it can be more helpful to notice your *intention* and your *direction* rather than your outcomes.

Intention and direction matter because they are about your heart. When you find yourself worrying about your success or lack thereof, dig a little deeper and inquire about your *intentions*. Do you intend to make progress in this area? If your answer is yes, then give yourself credit and keep moving. Likewise, check in about your *direction*. You may stumble and fall, but what path are you on and what direction are you facing? If you are still facing toward God, then you can simply get back up and keep walking.

When the desert fathers and mothers would counsel others, they would often suggest not judging or criticizing behavior. This is not to say we don't acknowledge when we are off track; we simply don't need to spend an inordinate amount of time wallowing in it or paying penance. We can seek to notice unhelpful thoughts or behaviors and then gently turn from them. Gently notice and then pivot.

Today, give yourself credit for what you truly intend in your heart. Is your heart's deepest longing for God himself? Acknowledge that and let your to dos flow from that place of connection with him. If you get tripped up, notice the direction you are headed. If you are still on your good path, don't judge or berate yourself. Simply get back up and keep walking. Your intention and direction matter and are foundational for whatever you do.

ADJUST YOUR VIEW OF TIME

The Stressed Achiever tries to make you feel pinched, as though you don't have time for what truly matters. The replenishing and relaxing activities easily get pushed to the side. It is this dynamic that can cause the stress to increase, becoming ever louder until you believe you have no choice at all in the matter. But here's the thing about time—we all have the same amount every day.

In our culture, we talk about moving at the pace of 24/7, but let's break it down even further. There are 10,080 minutes in a week and 1,440 minutes in each day. Is it really true that you can't capture any of those minutes for the people and tasks in your life that matter most, including soul care and self-care? Even if you believe that doing what matters is important, the Stressed Achiever, ever the taskmaster, won't allow you to do it in peace. This is why it is good to notice this voice, discern what's underneath her fears, and respond with grace.

The reality is we don't *have* time, we *make* time for what is important to us. It may feel like you don't have a choice over the matter, but, in many cases, you do. You can let go of this, postpone that, and delete that off your calendar for good. It may be true that we need to decrease the number of activities in our lives. But it is also true that we add weight to our lives by our own inner chatter. Shame, guilt, and perfectionism can make everything too heavy. As you notice and listen to the Stressed Achiever, you can become more free from her dynamics.

For many of us, there is a kind of breathlessness that accompanies our days. Pressures on the outside and the Stressed Achiever within can make for a perfect storm of overwhelm. There is time for everything that truly matters. The way we move and how we grow have a pace. Notice the Stressed Achiever, thank her for her loyal service, and then begin to manage your time and activities at the pace of grace as well as the pace of transformation.

To quell the overwhelm of the mind shift about time, try taking just one area of your life at a time. Beginning with work, what kinds of boundaries can you draw so that work doesn't seep into your evening or weekend life? You could try not checking email after 6:00 p.m. or on weekends. Or you could decide you have one day a week where you don't think about work at all. Even if your work is caring for others, there are ways to get some space for yourself. It does take some planning, but it is not impossible. Baby-sitters or elder sitters can come in the form of help from other family members or even paid help from time to time.

The cliché airplane illustration of "put your own oxygen mask on first" comes to mind. It's cliché because it is true. Putting on your own oxygen mask first is about making the time for you to refill and replenish so that you can continue to love, serve, and help the people in your life. Not doing so can lead to exhaustion, burnout, and even resentment.

Self-care is an important aspect of a healthy life. This may get shoved to the side because it seems selfish to do things for yourself. Get out your calendar and write in one self-care day per month, or even just one hour per week. During that time, your only job is to do something you love, something that refreshes you. Replenishing is important if we want to continue to thrive in our lives. The point is to begin. I invite you to take one area of your life and make one decision that shows you believe time is not your boss. All without pushing, trying, or angsting.

TELL IT LIKE IT IS

One of my favorite authors is Anne Lamott. I find her compelling because everything she writes contains an underlying honesty. She is unafraid to see and express the truth. Anne has made no secret about her recovery journey and I'm sure it plays a big part in her tendency toward raw candor. She tells the truth about her condition, and she isn't hiding behind gloss or glamor. She tells it like it is. My guess is that before she started telling the truth through her writing, she told the truth to herself. She faced her demons and overcame them by acknowledging their existence. Over the years, I have learned to look at myself in ways I never did before. I have grown accustomed to unearthing the deepest truth I can find. Bringing those places into the light, the presence of God, has been so freeing.

Sometimes, an overachieving voice is trying to keep us busy because it doesn't want us to feel our feelings. Feelings can be messy and sometimes it seems easier to just push them aside and pretend they aren't there. The over achiever in us often doesn't believe we can be loved for exactly who we are. The stripped-down version. The no frills version. No one could possibly love me apart from my achievements and productivity.

Acknowledging weakness and brokenness is not the first thing on the Stressed Achiever's to-do list. In fact, she will do whatever she can to hide both. But the process takes time. I had to walk into the shallow end of the pool and learn to make my way into the deep end. As I learned to tread water, I found that my fears subsided more and more. Instead of wanting to hide, I longed to dig, to go all the way down to the depths because freedom felt so good. Tell it like it is and embrace the healing that comes.

LIVING FROM FLOW

Just before we launched Unhurried Living, there was a vocational pressure building up inside of me. If this dynamic could be described as an image, I would say that I felt like a thoroughbred that was trapped in a stall with no freedom to move. Inwardly, I was raising up on my hind legs and whinnying loudly, but I couldn't figure out how to break free and run. I also felt like a fire hose with the spigot turned off. *If I could just turn the nozzle*, I thought, *water would come flooding out.* This is common among women who are entering the empty nest season. New energies emerge because there is a whole new world of time and space, and I was ready to go.

I decided to turn these images into a prayer: *God, I am open. How would you lead me to work in this season? Is there a position or role I could craft? Please show me the way. To get me rolling, could you please drop something in my lap so I could see the possibilities?* I know the last sentence of that prayer may seem silly or too bold, but I was desperate. Within a few months, my husband and I transitioned from our previous organization and founded Unhurried Living, which has become a beautiful place for me to share my life with others. The thoroughbred is now out of the stall, and the water is flowing freely.

I share this because it's okay to have an inner achiever. We want to express our God-given gifts. We desire to serve others. It's the *stressed* part that we can live without. We also don't want to let achievement define us. We don't have to *earn* who we are. We get to *express* who we are.

We know from my Italy story that I was not immune to the siren call of the Stressed Achiever. It was her voice that led to pushing, trying, and angsting, and, ultimately, an anxiety attack. She wanted to prove herself, and she didn't want to look dumb. She was determined to make things happen at a quicker pace. I am now happy to report that ever since the Florence Cathedral, I have not been under her spell in the same way. Do I still get triggered? Of course. But now I can more easily see when I am pushing and can make the adjustment quicker. And I am allowing myself to do this at the pace of transformation.

> We don't have to *earn* who we are. We get to *express* who we are.

MAKE THE LEAP

Some of you have stood on the edge of your own trust-precipice. You looked out and you couldn't see a thing, but you jumped anyway. You heard the call, and you took the leap. You have your own stories to tell of how God met you inwardly, in your deepest heart. You remember how God revealed himself to you in new ways because of your faith. God bless you for taking that leap.

If, however, you are standing at that metaphorical precipice right now, and fear is keeping you from leaping out in faith, it's okay. Take your time. God is patient. God simply longs for you to know that he sees your deepest desires and most inward hopes, and he will walk with you in your next season of growth. Know this: you will be caught. Your troubles may not fade away, but you will have the assurance of a loving God who honors your leap of faith. Your soul will soar, the voice of the Stressed Achiever will begin to fade, and you will be that much closer to your truest self.

Practices for the Stressed Achiever

Remember that Jesus includes you among his friends. Let this inform your sense of value and worth. Say to yourself, "I am beloved."

Set healthy boundaries around your work engagements. Decide when and how often to check email and social media and how often you have appointments. Give yourself the gift of buffer time within your calendar.

Choose self-care. Calendar this time and be sure it includes something you love and that replenishes you.

NOTICE, DISCERN, AND RESPOND

Notice

- How does the Stressed Achiever show up in your relationships and responsibilities?

Discern

- How have you come to rely on the Stressed Achiever in ways that aren't helpful?

Respond

- When have you taken your own leap of faith? What was the process and outcome?

- What would it look like for you to relax into the space of the B+? What might be the benefits of easing up a bit?

- What is your version of the thoroughbred trapped in the stall? How are you longing to express your gifts these days?

4

From Positive Thinker to Growing in Hope

YOU MAY BE WONDERING WHY a positive sounding voice is mingling in with voices that sound a little more intense. It's because unhelpful thinking doesn't always skew negative. *Everything will work out. It probably wasn't meant to be anyway. You should probably distract yourself until this blows over. Now we can move on to something new!* What could possibly be wrong with thinking positively about a difficult situation? It's better than sinking down into the hole of pessimism. Okay, I'll give you that. But I'd like to argue that positive thinking is the lowest rung when compared with optimism and hope. And we can do so much better than the bottom rung.

THE VOICE OF THE POSITIVE THINKER

Positive thinking has a Scarlett O'Hara fiddle-dee-dee undertone to it. Reality is calling, but rather than listen, you pick up your dress, turn in a huff, and begin to walk out the door. But not before you stop in your tracks, slowly turn your bonnet-laden head, and sneer at reality one last time. The determined look in your eye says, *I'm sure it will all work out just fine . . . because that's the way I want it to!* Cut again to the huffing and leaving. Mere positive thinking, at its worst, can develop into denial, and that is nowhere near the path of transformation. Thomas Merton says it this way: "There is no greater disaster in the spiritual life than to be immersed in unreality."[1]

A phrase I hear often these days is "toxic positivity." It's the idea that no matter how bad things get, you should always maintain a positive mindset. It's like living with a nonstop Beach Boys album playing in the background. "I'm picking up good vibrations. . . . Oh my, my what a sensation. . . . Oh my, my what elation. . . . good, good, good, good vibrations."[2] This is great for a day at the beach, but it is no way to live. As we grow and mature, it is necessary to face the sad, unfair, and traumatic circumstances of our lives and to make our way to greater healing. Toxic positivity does not lead to wholeness. Rather, it is a path to pretending and denial.

I spent many years of my life dancing to the beat of the undiscerned Positive Thinker. Positive thinking does make you upbeat, but it's the dynamic of denial that makes this a truly unhelpful mode. It kept me from being sad. It hindered me from expressing anger. I would push against people who were sarcastic or depressed, not wanting to bring the tone of my inner party down. The rub is that not feeling your sadness or anger usually manifests as something else and, for me, that was anxiety. One time, in my early twenties, I experienced some unexpected chest pain. I went to the doctor only to run into an incredulous look and some sarcastic mention of managing stress. There was nothing physical about my pain, but that was no excuse for her poor bedside manner. Surprised and a bit confused, I simply took her exasperated commentary on my mental state and left the building. The voice of the Positive Thinker in me didn't even really take it in. I didn't have the tools to make any headway with her diagnosis. So, like Scarlett, I fiddle-dee-dee'd my way back into my life.

OPTIMISM AND HOPE

Positive thinking may be a fine place to begin, but we are invited to much more. Out beyond positive thinking is optimism. Optimism is more helpful because it is grounded in reality. It's not looking for an easy answer or to deny what is actually occurring. Optimism doesn't lose heart, and it continues to look for actual possibilities. It's keeping your chin up in the best possible way. According to author and inspirational speaker Simon Sinek, "Optimism is the ability to focus on where we are going, not where we are coming from."[3]

Imagine you are standing in the middle of the road and using your binoculars to get a distant view. You can't make out exactly what is there, but you see enough to know that this is the way to go. Optimism is that thing that reminds you to pull out your binoculars to look in the first place. It's enough inner "yes" to believe something good may be out there. You can't predict the future, and you don't know precisely how it will turn out, but optimism is what moves us toward the deepest form: hope.

Hope is a dynamic that lives way beneath the surface. It's in that center place in between your heart and your gut. It's a kind of *knowing*. I am an optimist by nature, and I skew easily toward multiple possibilities. But there was a time, a while back, when it seemed that my bent toward optimism had been put to sleep. That may not sound like a big deal, but for someone who enjoys the shinier ways of thinking, lack of optimism can descend slowly into depression and then hopelessness. And hopelessness is a rough dynamic from which to emerge. It was during this optimism-lights-out that I encountered a major shift in my understanding of the difference between optimism and hope. Optimism is still a good thing, but it can rely on circumstance, feelings, and drive. Again, not necessarily a bad thing. But when there is no life preserver of good feelings to pull you into the boat, even optimism can have a hard time keeping you from drifting out to sea.

The invitation for me was to a deeper sense of hope. Hope is beyond circumstance, emotion, and, might I dare say, will. Hope is a profound connection to the love and presence of God. Hope comes from drawing on the well of past faithfulness of God in your life. He took care of me then, and I know he will do the same now. This kind of hope emerges from that center place within you, and you usually only hear it when you are listening carefully. Or, like me, when faced with the desperation of no other choice. *You can only reach for something deeper when you lose your grasp on what you already know.* How else would you be urged to search for something more unless there was a deficit of some kind? This kind of hope does not shout. It is a beautiful, quiet roar that burns within. You . . . just . . . know.

> You can only reach for something deeper when you lose your grasp on what you already know.

Positive thinking is a place to start, as long as you don't let it devolve into denial. But I encourage you not to park there. Optimism is great for possibility, momentum, and confident action. Hope comes from your core and is typically the fruit of the light going out somewhere in your life. Hope as an engine is unstoppable because it cannot be deterred from its mission to see you through to the end. Hope reminds you that you are loved and cared for no matter what is occurring around you.

Now that we have been reminded of a deeper hope, we can settle into an uncomfortable reality. Hope is matured by being tested just like any other good solid virtue or gift. Hope is so deep that it can only be accessed when you are pushed to your limits—the earth is shifting beneath your feet, or the sky feels like it is falling, or there is just a single rope dangling from above. In times like this, we must dig in for something more. Positive thinking or even optimism are not enough in these situations.

In *Thoughts in Solitude*, Thomas Merton states,

> The desert was the region in which the Chosen People had wandered for forty years, cared for by God alone. They could have reached the Promised Land in a few months if they had traveled directly to it. God's plan was that they should learn to love him in the wilderness and that they should always look back upon the time in the desert as the idyllic time of their life with him alone. The desert was created simply to be itself, not to be transformed by [people] into something else.[4]

The wilderness is the geography whereby the Positive Thinker can move to optimism and ultimately hope. The wilderness is the deepening experience where we sink into God alone. It is the purifying reality.

> The wilderness is the geography whereby the Positive Thinker can move to optimism and ultimately hope.

EMMA'S POSITIVE THINKER

Emma is a glowing and vibrant woman who loves growing and reaching for what God has for her. She serves many in individual and group coaching as well as being a conference and retreat speaker. Her heart overflows with love for others, and she finds great joy in sharing her wealth of knowledge and wisdom.

Emma has a strong connection to the Positive Thinker. In her case, the Positive Thinker manifested by a determined uplifting thought: *I can make this happen.* Different from confidence, this thought can sometimes lead to unhelpful pushing, trying, or angsting, and, when someone else is involved, can make for an uncomfortable relational connection. Emma's story is rooted in a longtime friendship that changed over time. Her friend was a high achiever with a corporate job that included all of the perks. However, their friendship began to suffer when her friend got this new job. With all of these new responsibilities as well as teaching night classes after work at a local university, Emma's friend pulled back, and the friendship began to fade. This disconnection deeply affected Emma, and she felt hurt and abandoned. She longed for the earlier version of the friendship, and her perception was that her friend no longer wanted that.

Emma's issue with positive thinking manifested itself in the determination that this situation would indeed work out the way she wanted. So much so that she took her perception of the dynamics of the situation and, ironically, turned the negativity back on herself. Her positive spin—*this will work out and I will find a way*—led to her taking the blame, and then, of course, more unhelpful thoughts followed. That's the thing about the Positive Thinker. It might begin with what appears to be a positive thought, "The change I want is possible, and I will work this out!" But any number of dynamics arise within us and begin to move us down a circuitous path that may not be the healthiest for us.

Emma began to question every interaction. If her friend didn't connect, Emma was sure she had done something wrong. She became hypercritical, judgmental, and she over thought every single interaction. She persisted in this type of thinking until it culminated in a most triggering thought: *I am being rejected.* This was the beginning of a wilderness experience for her, and it was followed by a flood of thoughts:

Why do I try? I'm always disappointed. But I have to keep trying.

She doesn't want a relationship with me.

What's wrong with me? I have great relationships with other friends, so what's the deal here?

She doesn't need me.

It was that last thought, *she doesn't need me,* that felt like a slap in the face. Emma described it as a wake-up call. That thought slammed the brakes on the energy of positivity she was using to keep pushing forward. Even if it was not true that her friend didn't need her, it was the beginning of Emma pivoting to the search for a healthier way to address her situation. As it turned out, Emma's perceptions were not true. Her friend did want the friendship, she simply wasn't able to figure out how to manage it all. But Emma still had some more inner work to do before she would see this clearly.

It was about this time that I, as Emma's soul care coach, shared with her the spiritual practice of NDR. There were a few questions in the *discern* part of the practice that shone a bright light on Emma's thinking, and she was able to gain some clarity. Here are a few of the discernment questions that helped her:

Does this thought sound like a friend or an enemy?

When you speak the word out loud, does it affirm or degrade?

What would it sound like if you spoke these thoughts to someone else?
What was the tone of the thought?

Emma found that the new experience of saying her thoughts out loud led to refreshed thinking. She could hear the tone, which made discerning the thought so much easier. When our thoughts are silent, ricocheting inside our brains, they make so much sense. However, when we speak our thoughts out loud, the masks come off and you can see them for what they are.

Armed with a renewed vision, Emma was able to make her way to some new and more helpful thoughts. She found that she was more easily resting in God's presence. This was not new to her; however, she was able to dig in deeper for the love she longed for, and she relaxed into that space. From there, she learned not to be a "mind reader" and to allow God to help her interpret situations. In a time of journaling and prayer, she received the encouragement, "You can have hope beyond hopelessness. God is the way to get there." This is what makes hope *hope*. It is a critical shift for the Positive Thinker. Moving out of mistaken perceptions, through the pain of hopelessness, and all the way through to hope. Hope is grounding and gives you a solid place to stand.

Emma looked herself square in the eye and saw that she was being self-centered and needy. Her trying was tied to her deep desire for esteem and affection from her friend. From there, she was able to embrace a mindset of grace. Listening prayer, self-reflection, and journaling were crucial to this transition. Emma now more often lives in the light in relationship to her friend. God helped her get out of her familiar pattern, and it became easier once she let the pressure off. Her friend responded by leaning into the space created by Emma's easing up. They now have a more open relationship of care and love.

Our own Positive Thinker can cause us to push, try, or angst our way forward until we hit our own brick wall. And, like Emma, our invitation is to notice our unhelpful thoughts, discern what they are up to, and respond in new, more mature ways.

HUMAN, MENTIONABLE, MANAGEABLE

As I write the first draft of this book, we are about one year into the Covid-19 worldwide pandemic. This has been a year unlike any other in my life. The waves of information, misinformation, and emotion have overwhelmed most of us throughout the year. From stockpiling toilet paper to masks to social distancing, what we thought of as normal is now a distant dot in our rearview mirror. One day, in the first few weeks of the pandemic, it hit me that this was more serious than I had originally thought. At first, it all felt very far away, and we still believed it would pass quickly. On that day, however, I watched a news segment and found myself growing more alarmed. "This is serious now. We need to go grocery shopping for supplies!" I exclaimed to Alan. We got into the car and drove to one of the more expensive specialty grocery stores in our area. I'm still not sure why I chose such a high-end market. We proceeded to dash through the store, filling our cart with pantry items that would last in case we were closed up in our homes and unable to go out again. From organic beef jerky to ridiculously expensive canned tuna, I was armed for the worst. Of course, all grocery stores remained open, and I have been able to shop any time I wanted for this entire year. And we've now come to jokingly call my pantry stash "panic tuna" and "emergency jerky." It was still sitting on our shelf months later.

Fear is one of the driving forces of the Positive Thinker. The positivity is there to hide the fear of what is happening outwardly and inwardly. During a pandemic, it is good for all of us to stay responsibly informed and healthy, helping to keep others safe as well. It's also okay to feel fear, anger, frustration, or confusion. But glossing over all of this with positivity is ultimately unhelpful, and fear is not our best motivator nor our best engine.

The Mr. Rogers movie, *A Beautiful Day in the Neighborhood*, came out the year before the pandemic. Like most people, I found the movie compelling and engaging. It was not at all what I expected, which was a welcome treat. One of my favorite lines from the movie was this: "Anything that's human is mentionable. And anything that is mentionable can be more manageable."[5] Fear is definitely a human emotion—which, by Mr. Rogers's definition, means that it is mentionable and, by extension, more manageable.

The Positive Thinker is quelled when we learn to notice our fear and mention it to someone, even if that someone is ourselves. Positivity can keep things buried. Mentioning brings the issues to the surface so they can be looked at and managed. Learn to share with your trusted friends or loved ones how you feel so that you can manage your fears, worries, and concerns. Not in a "dump it on them" way, but in an "I need to process something with you" way. "Dumping" has no purpose. It is unloading without thoughtfulness or care for healing. "Processing," on the other hand, is a healthy part of our growth. This might seem nuanced, but it is an important distinction. Is your end goal to simply vent or to be healed? A safe, lovingly detached friend; spiritual director; or soul care coach would be able to hold space for you while you process. Sharing our feelings can keep them from overwhelming us. Our feelings want to be seen and heard and it doesn't work to deny them. Then we, as the mature adults we are, can continue to discern our responses.

Mr. Rogers had such a lovely way about him. But there was an intense drive under the surface. He was tenaciously good. The way he engaged teaching children about the real current affairs of the world, well, he was singular in his efforts. You could say he was a Positive Thinker, but it wouldn't take you long to see that his convictions were much deeper than that, moving through to optimism and ultimately, hope.

This idea of human-mentionable-manageable really brings it all into focus. It's an invitation to acknowledge what is really going on and to speak it. What we mention is manageable. This can help the Positive Thinker to calm a bit, so she won't be afraid to move forward in more healthy ways. Mr. Rogers's statement encourages us not to hide. What are you thinking or feeling today? What can you mention about it? How might that make it more manageable? Human. Mentionable. Manageable. This process is just the shift the Positive Thinker needs.

THE SUFFERING CHRIST

In my home, I am famous for creating piles of paper for those "just in case" moments. A few years ago, I uncovered a humble scrap of paper in one of these legendary piles. On it was scrawled the record of medication I took to quell the throbbing pain down my left leg caused by a disc extrusion in my spine. This was what I ingested over the course of two days:

8:30 a.m.—pain pill

11:30 a.m.—four ibuprofen

1:00 p.m.—pain pill

3:15 p.m.—four ibuprofen

5:30 p.m.—pain pill

8:00 p.m.—four ibuprofen

11:00 p.m.—pain pill

2:30 a.m.—pain pill

5:30 a.m.—four ibuprofen

8:30 a.m.—pain pill

12:00 p.m.—six ibuprofen

3:30 p.m.—pain pill

7:00 p.m.—six ibuprofen

10:30 p.m.—pain pill

All this medication and I was still moaning out loud in pain. These pills simply numbed me just enough so that I could bear to be in my body. I am not exaggerating. Nerve pain is that bad. Those first two weeks were excruciating. Until we could find out what was wrong and decide on a treatment, I was left with pills to help take the edge off. It was the worst physical pain of my life.

At the time, I didn't know how the pain would come to an end. I was distressed at how much pain medication I was taking, but it was unbearable otherwise. It was the pain that wouldn't be consoled. Every three hours, I was taking medication that barely began to touch the severity of the throbbing. Living with pain, for any length of time, changes you. There's no room for positive thinking in the dark and scary forest of severe pain.

Alan would drive me to my daily chiropractic appointments for decompression therapy. It was all I could do to get in the van. I felt as though I were wearing blinders as everything around me dimmed in comparison to the pain. Every single time, upon my arrival, one of the doctors would say cheerily, "Hi! How are you doing today?!" In my mind I was wondering why in the world he would ask such a question. I wanted to spew, "How do you think I am?! I'm in the worst pain of my life and it is not letting up! Why are you asking me such a stupid question?" But instead, I simply replied, "I'm okay."

The Positive Thinker tries to protect itself from pain. But it is actually the darkness and suffering that brings about the maturity the Positive Thinker requires to move to hope. Jesus himself suffered unimaginably, and it is by connecting with the suffering Christ that we grow, deepen, and become more whole. This is a difficult truth because no one likes pain. But hardship bears the fruit of vulnerability, courage, and, ultimately, hope.

> Jesus himself suffered unimaginably, and it is by connecting with the suffering Christ that we grow, deepen, and become more whole.

LOVE POURED OUT

Pound! Pound! Pound! What is that sound? I awake from an afternoon nap.[6] Someone is hammering nails into thick wood, and it is echoing throughout the grounds of a local retreat center. I was helping to facilitate a leadership retreat, and I worried that the other retreat participants would dislike the noise during their afternoon Unhurried Time with God. I finally realized there were two gentlemen continuing to add to the new Stations of the Cross—a series of paintings that depict the journey Jesus took to the cross. They were nailing wood ties to line the path, and I was wishing I had requested no such noise be allowed during our solitude day.

Hammering and solitude do not go together.

Then the irony strikes me. I am bothered by the sounds of a hammer and nails. Is it possible that Jesus was "bothered" by that sound as they nailed him to the cross? The sound echoed throughout the grounds and my heart. Jesus was brutally pierced for all of us. *Oh, those bothersome nails! Stop the pounding!* He must have thought the same thing: *Stop the pounding!* But he had already done business with the Father in the garden. He had already asked for the cup to be removed. And now the cup was being broken and poured out. The agony. The pounding. Experiencing these pounding sounds in a time alone with God began to make sense. The hammer pounding nails into wood is exactly the sound that helps wake me up to the depths of Jesus' love.

I decided to walk over to the Stations of the Cross and make my way along the path. When I encountered the image of Jesus' beaten body, I noticed something unique. Out of all fourteen images, it was the only image where Jesus' eyes were open wide and looking at the viewer. I imagined him saying, *My eyes are wide open. I know what I am doing.* As I made my way to a nearby bench a poem flowed from within:

Eyes wide open
Gazing into my soul
Love poured out
Burning pain
Ultimate sacrifice
Pursuing love
I am yours.

What is the medicine that soothes the Positive Thinker? A good dose of real, sacrificial love that guides us ever so graciously to the doorway of hope. Don't let the lowest rung of positive thinking keep you from experiencing hope in all its fullness. Let yourself experience the unbearable parts of your life with the raw pain of it all. Jesus suffered in the past and he suffers with you now, here in the present. Let this kind of presence and grace change you. Let it lead to a deep well of hope as you live your life with more intention, wisdom, and grace.

Practices for the Positive Thinker

Remember that you are a human being. And humans are allowed to have off days. It's okay to talk about your hurts and weaknesses with God and with trusted friends.

Think of a place of pain in your life. It may be physical or emotional pain. Take a moment to remember that this might be a doorway to greater maturity and hope.

Take a moment to see Jesus as the ultimate wounded healer. Jesus knows what it is like to suffer. Spend a couple of minutes enjoying his empathy and presence.

NOTICE, DISCERN, AND RESPOND

Notice

- How does the Positive Thinker typically express itself in your life?

Discern

- How does the Positive Thinker keep you stuck?

Respond

- Where do you find yourself on the spectrum of positive thinking, optimism, and hope? How might your movement toward hope increase?

- What is one area of your life that you have deemed unmentionable? With whom might you mention it and bring it into the light?

- How might you connect with the loving gaze of Christ crucified? How does this move you toward hope?

5

From Inner Critic to Gaining Fresh Perspective

ONE SUNNY MORNING, a small group of women and I were enjoying time together outside a coffee shop. One of the women began to describe her current relationship with God. She talked about it as though it were something she had "been neglecting" and "needed to get back into." She referenced "being in the Word" and other practices from the "good Christian to-do list." She did not use the term "good Christian," but that was the spirit in which she shared her story. She had "not been doing well." And she would "get better in the new year" because she was going to "start back up again."

Why am I picking apart her phrasing? Because words matter. And the thoughts and feelings behind them matter. Do you hear the undercurrent of the voice of the Inner Critic in this woman's description of her relationship with God? The Inner Critic is, of course, concerned with whether things are good or bad. These phrases all have meaning because they reveal her unconscious belief that a with-God life, at its center, is made of the tasks she has set up to determine how she is doing. There was a separateness inherent in the way she described her relationship with God. It seemed to be built on the belief that God was somewhere else and that she was disconnected and needed to find a way to be near again. She is not alone. I've seen this before in my conversations with women. And I have been that woman myself.

THE VOICE OF THE INNER CRITIC

The Inner Critic can look and sound like the character Miranda Priestly, the head of a fashion magazine from the movie *The Devil Wears Prada*.[1] Lips always pursed. Eyes constantly ready to squint in judgment. Always put out. *You really messed that up. Why can't you get this right? Couldn't you have done better than that? Why do you always keep me waiting? Things could be so much better than this. You don't look-sound-smell right. Fix it!*

Miranda's dry perfectionism is consistently directed at the protagonist, Andrea Sachs. After giving new hire Andrea (Andy) the once over, Miranda states, "I see you have no interest in fashion." Andy tries to correct her, and Miranda abruptly cuts her off, as she lowers her glasses and proceeds to slowly look up and down Andy's frumpy-clothed body, "No, no. That wasn't a question." Later, as Miranda waits for Andy to hand her some paperwork, Miranda says, "By all means, move at a glacial pace. You know how that thrills me." And, when Miranda is berating her first assistant over a botched appointment, she calmly seethes, "Details of your incompetence do not interest me."

Your Inner Critic may or may not be as cold as this, but she is likely as perfectionistic, disgruntled, and judgmental. The sad part is, the Inner Critic isn't always aimed outward like Miranda's. It is often aimed at ourselves, and it clangs in our heads like a nonstop gong. *Do better. Be more. And it had better be perfect!*

YOU ARE ALREADY GOOD

Isn't there so much more to this thing we call the Christian life than doing the right things so that we can get credit and feel better about ourselves?

Yes! Overwhelmingly, yes.

It's easy, but unintentional, to think the Christian life is merely about following rules (implicit and explicit) that have been given to us. From there, we may slide into praising ourselves for following the rules or judging ourselves—and others—for breaking them. This includes the church's clichéd guidelines: quiet time, church attendance, tithing, and going on a mission trip to a foreign country. Add to that the demand to be the perfect wife, mother, or friend, and you have an overwhelming burden not meant for you to carry. These dynamics can become measuring sticks that shift our focus away from the God-breathed relationship and process that is already ours.

At the start, many of us were invited into "a personal relationship with Jesus Christ." Then, somehow, this devolved into to-do and to-don't lists, and the relational aspect fell to the sidelines. I live in a can-do, fast-paced culture that highly values productivity. Many of us have been hardwired to earn what we get and to make sure we grab attention when we've done a good job. But see how insidious this is if it flows into how we talk about our relationship with God? We reduce God to a task, and we break him down into subtasks so that we can measure ourselves and come up winners. The Inner Critic loves tasks and rules because then it has something to criticize, condemn, or measure. Most of us do not have any relationships in our lives that are only measured by the to-dos, checklists, and tasks that are involved. What would that look like in a friendship or a marriage? *There is no vibrant life in a relationship that is only measured by tasks accomplished.*

Let's take a pause here for a moment. I'm not saying that our spiritual practices are merely tasks and that they are unnecessary. Exactly the opposite. Spiritual practices are indispensable. At their best, they are a pathway into further connection with God. But they are the stones on which we step; they are not the destination. And since *in him we live and move and have our being* (Acts 17:28), we don't need to travel far. God is near. God is here. God is within. We can remember what we already have and, more importantly, whose we already are. It is God we seek and that is the point. The practice or activity is not the thing. God is the thing. See the difference?

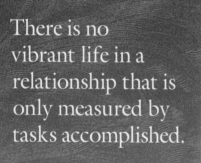

There is no vibrant life in a relationship that is only measured by tasks accomplished.

Seeing this difference can open a world of encounter. More things count than we realize. Recall my "top of the Florence Cathedral" experience. I was looking out over the rooftops, trying to locate excitement, as though it were an outside commodity. The Spirit gently reminded me that I could shift my gaze to the moment and choose gratitude. That quiet focus changed my heart and my experience. God saw me and God was with me. I was soaking in the nurturing presence of God just as much as I would have in a traditional quiet time. This was an invitation further into the with-God life.

Imagine my life as a pearl necklace. My lifeline is the string I hold in my hands. As I make my way through the years, I notice how God meets me within each experience. In a process of looking back and discerning, I engage a narrative that includes God's work *in* me.

This becomes a pearl that I place on my string. Over the course of weeks, months, and years, I build rows of pearls to which I can return, to make sense of my current season, or to merely give thanks. I remind myself of God's faithfulness and the trajectory I am on. There is a stability that occurs as this pearl necklace becomes a grounding place, elements of my life woven together in one beautiful and precious piece.

Therefore, it is good to have the long view in mind. Measuring by minutes, hours, and days just isn't enough, and the Inner Critic loves to sneak in to remind you that you aren't making headway nearly fast enough. Having a long view can quiet this voice because you are measuring growth over months and years. The long view also reminds us that we are human beings. We are not machines that can endlessly crank out a product. We are more a fruit tree than a widget factory.

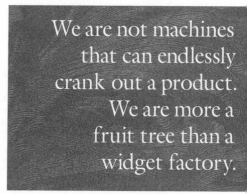

> We are not machines that can endlessly crank out a product. We are more a fruit tree than a widget factory.

Your own life-pearl necklace is a way you can stay connected to what God is doing in you and through you, one situation at a time. Place each life pearl on the strand and collect them all. How do you see your story unfolding? How do you notice your connection to God being strengthened? Tracking your story *with God* brings far more freedom than rules, measuring sticks, and judging. This is so different from "things you do" to "keep on track" and "prove you are growing." Your very life, inner and outer work, becomes the masterpiece that it is. The real measure of our goodness is already established in Psalm 139:13-18 (*The Message*):

Oh yes, you shaped me first inside, then out;
you formed me in my mother's womb.
I thank you, High God—you're breathtaking!
Body and soul, I am marvelously made!
I worship in adoration—what a creation!
You know me inside and out,
you know every bone in my body;
You know exactly how I was made, bit by bit,
how I was sculpted from nothing into something.
Like an open book, you watched me grow from conception
to birth;
all the stages of my life were spread out before you,
The days of my life all prepared
before I'd even lived one day.
Your thoughts—how rare, how beautiful!
God, I'll never comprehend them!
I couldn't even begin to count them—
any more than I could count the sand of the sea.
Oh, let me rise in the morning and live always with you!

Do not confuse the Inner Critic's good girl to-do list with your
progress or your value. You already have what you need. You are
good. You are loved. You can establish this in your own mind and
then continue to move out from that place in any and every season
of life.

AVA'S INNER CRITIC

During her first half of life, Ava would describe her life as working
well. She was disciplined, volunteering in ministry, and she was an
involved mom providing care for her family. Her driving belief was
that God would bless her if she did it all right. In fact, this became

a mantra: *Do it right. God will bless you.* Her Inner Critic never let up. She had the answers for just about everything. She could tell you how to correct your wrongs and improve your rights. By age forty-five, she had been in therapy four times in hopes of improving herself. Her central question was, "What am I doing wrong, because *they* aren't changing?" The Inner Critic was aimed at herself because she couldn't figure out how to get through to others. It never occurred to her that she might be perceived as critical or judgmental. She did not want to be criticized, yet she was criticizing everyone else with her "I have a better idea" attitude.

All of this caused bitterness and resentment to build up, but she would never let it show. Growing up, her mother told her anger is not attractive, so Ava was determined to keep it hidden. She simply carried on with the assumption that perfection was important and doing things right would be rewarded with affirmation. Unfortunately, fear of other people's opinions was an overwhelming layer that got added to the mix. Ava was deeply afraid that people, and even God, would back away. She believed God's stance toward her was, *Pull it together and I'll come back when you are ready.* Or, *you're doing this again?* In Ava's mind, God could not be pleased. She was driven by the Inner Critic to do better and do more. The Inner Critic often shows up to "help" us be perfect—or at least good.

As you can imagine, Ava's Inner Critic was plentiful, with an endless list of judgments and corrections:

You are selfish and self-absorbed.
You did not do a good job of loving.
I'm a good person if . . .
Just do it. It's the right way. Don't ask questions.
Do it right. God will bless you.
Other people's opinions matter very much.

It's not good enough.

There is one right way to do this, and I know what it is.

Peace of mind cannot be right when so much is wrong.

But the most pervasive voices for Ava were these:

You are good when you do the right things perfectly.

That's not quite good enough.

Try harder. Do better.

Ava's movement from this way of thinking was gradual. Discontentment and restlessness in her marriage led her to seek help as she didn't know how to cope with the hardships that engulfed her. In addition, her son's struggle with addiction was increasing, and her attempts to fix this led her into a state of deep sadness, fear, and frustration. Happiness eluded her and nothing felt light as she lost her sense of humor and began to isolate.

This was the precursor to her inner shift. She had reached a new level of not being able to fix herself, her son, her husband, or anyone else. The certainty she clung to before had completely vanished and she sunk into sadness. She felt as though she should be able to manage, but her ability waned. The weight of feeling like a failure as a parent was crushing, so much so that she found herself in the fetal position. *If only I would have loved my son better this would not have happened.* This unfixable situation was a brick wall of non-resolution.

Ava's turning point was met with a radical vision of a new way to live. During an Al-Anon meeting, a woman shared the story of her daughter's addiction that caused her to leap from a moving vehicle, resulting in a crushed ankle. Ava watched in amazement as this woman shared her story without being curled up in a ball. The woman was functional, and it sparked Ava's search to learn how to be lovingly detached. The woman's daughter was out of control, and yet the woman was hanging in there, relaxed and hopeful. Ava wondered how this was possible. This was a level of acceptance Ava did not yet have access to, and a new way was opening before her.

As she pressed deeper into this new way forward, a refreshed world of thoughts emerged for Ava:

I can change my thinking.

Keep an open mind.

Let it be enough.

Easy does it.

There is more than one way to do things.

You may be right.

Even though these new thoughts were welcome, Ava felt like she was betraying God by laying down her search for goodness and perfection. But she slowly pressed on as she learned to stop critiquing herself and others. She learned to act the opposite from what she did before as a new level of self-awareness opened to her. Acceptance of situations grew over time, and she did not carry as much anger or resentment. Her equation of "worry equals love" began to fade, and God granted her the inner peace she so desperately longed for. She learned to say *I don't know* and to embrace mystery more easily, as pushing, trying, and angsting took a back seat. She took time to see her assets and gifts through the lens of gratitude rather than obligation and performance.

These days, Ava chooses to make the continuous adjustments necessary to move through life while her Inner Critic has its proper place at the table. She doesn't feel the need to be perfectly on course at all times.

Here are a few more new thoughts that keep her moving in her chosen direction:

Progress, not perfection.

Easy does it.

How important is it?

Would you rather be right, or would you rather be happy?

The Inner Critic is absolutely positive she knows what is right and what she can do to fix it. She is trying to help keep you safe and we can thank her for how hard she works at that. *True freedom is found in our ability to accept what is occurring around us.* It is letting others live the way they want to live while making our own choices in the midst. It is releasing judgment when we see something off-kilter. When a thought pops up into Ava's mind that reminds her of a truth that she's resisting, she gives God credit for the goodness. When a person agitates her and she is able to accept them as they are, she sees it as a gift from God. She used to be locked in righteous anger, but now she experiences this less and less. Ava considers it a miracle that she is freer from the Inner Critic. God's loving power is greater than her own, and she is fine with that.

THROW THE FIRST STONE

The Inner Critic gains energy from the negative input we receive over the course of our lives. Cruel school children, a harsh parent, or a vindictive boss can add fuel to our own inner chatter regarding our value or worth. There is a woman in the Gospels who might understand our plight. John 8:1-11 opens with Jesus at the temple. A group of self-righteous men were trying to trick Jesus, and using this woman was the worst part of their scheme. The public shaming and extreme treatment were uncalled for. But Jesus, in true form, took the time to skillfully (with the men) and lovingly (with the woman) put everyone in their place.

Let's not get started on why the woman was brought into this pseudo-court without the man with whom she had an affair. Adding to this, the men brought up the law itself, stating that women like this were to be stoned. Can you imagine what this woman was feeling? Dragged and pushed along, paraded out in public as others shine a light on her worst moment. The men had no regard for her as a person. They simply wanted to trap Jesus, and she was the latest casualty in their plot to take him down.

Stories like this make me love Jesus so much. He always saw people for who they were. The self-righteous were put in their place, and the wounded were healed. Consistently. The story continued with Jesus bending down and using his finger to write on the ground. The religious leaders kept pressing him, causing Jesus to utter this genius statement as he continued to write, "Let any one of you who is without sin be the first to throw a stone at her" (John 8:7). Jesus gave them the chance to look within. For the first time in the story, the men got real and had to admit that they, too, were not perfect. In their cruelty and trickery, they took pause and had to admit that they were not without sin. Even though they left disgruntled, reality hit them square in the eye, and they had no choice but to drop their stones and leave. It certainly feels like too little, too late. However, they did the right thing by realizing they were not perfect. Jesus then lovingly turned to the woman, "Woman, where are they? Has no one condemned you?" "No one, sir," she said. "Then neither do I condemn you," Jesus declared (John 8:10-11).

Our Inner Critic takes turns at where she directs her accusations. Sometimes she is the self-righteous leader trying to dig in and make a point against others. Sometimes she directs all of her fury inward with a tirade of negativity and shame. But let's borrow the love and grace of Jesus toward the woman in this story. We can learn to provide the same level-headedness he offered to the men and the grace offered to the woman. We can receive for ourselves, "neither do I condemn you." Notice how this might help calm the Inner Critic.

When the Inner Critic wants to berate you for your past, citing all the ways you didn't get it right, remember this: every version of yourself got you to where you are right now. It may have been a rocky road; however, you can thank each version of yourself for being who she was at the time. It is how you got here. And whether or not you are satisfied with wherever *here* is, you've made it this far. And you can choose what to do going forward.

Remember, the Inner Critic, as with all voices, is merely doing her best to grant us a sense of safety or protection. And we can sincerely thank the Inner Critic for her help as we learn to notice and befriend her. As we continue to sit at the head of our inner dining table, we can let the Inner Critic know that she can relax and that we can handle things in ways that serve us well.

PLACE YOUR LIFE BEFORE GOD

The Inner Critic is my go-to when I am tired or stressed. I easily roll down the hill of judgment and blame when I am in one of my moods. Grace fades into the distance, and I fall into unhelpful thinking. Anger, bitterness, and resentment are all waiting for me at the bottom of the hill and down into the valley. What helps me recover from this free fall? I can remember that the Inner Critic keeps me from receiving what God is offering. God is bringing out the best in me, and I can help expand that fullness by allowing the Inner Critic to be transformed.

So here's what I want you to do, God helping you: Take your everyday, ordinary life—your sleeping, eating, going-to-work, and walking-around life—and place it before God as an offering. Embracing what God does for you is the best thing you can do for him. Don't become so well-adjusted to your culture that you fit into it without even thinking. Instead, fix your attention on God. You'll be changed from the inside out. Readily recognize what he wants from you, and quickly respond to it. Unlike the culture around you, always dragging you down to its level of immaturity, *God brings the best out of you, develops well-formed maturity in you.* I'm speaking to you out of deep gratitude for all that God has given me, and especially as I have responsibilities in relation to you. Living then, as every one of you does, in pure grace, *it's important that you not misinterpret yourselves as people who are bringing this goodness to God. No, God brings it all to you. The only accurate way to understand ourselves is by what God is and by what he does for us, not by what we are and what we do for him.* (Romans 12:1-3 *The Message*, emphasis mine)

The Inner Critic wants to judge, manage, and fix. Our true self longs to receive and express, not control. God is bringing out the best in us. God develops maturity in us. It is not what we do for God. And it is certainly not giving the Inner Critic the wheel that helps us to achieve what we already have. God is the great initiator, and we are responders. This is sheer gift. We accept and agree with God. If I can agree with the way the loving Trinity sees and loves me, then I can more naturally love myself and offer that same love to others.

GAIN SOME PERSPECTIVE

You know that beautiful moment when you take off in an airplane and you begin to rise above the

> God is the great initiator, and we are responders.

earth? Rather quickly the buildings minimize, and the vehicles turn into toy cars. Your perspective shifts as you see miles and miles of homes, knowing they represent thousands of people. The wealthy, the poor, the happy, the sad—you can't distinguish between them at 3,000 feet. It is an opportunity for problems to shrink. As you continue to fly out over the shoreline to the ocean, you see the pounding waves that normally knock you over. Now they are thin, white, squiggly lines, barely noticeable.

As you achieve your cruising altitude of about 35,000 feet, the homes and buildings are small dots, and you cannot distinguish between individual trees. Only the broadest paint strokes of nature are visible. The peaks and valleys of mountains, the ocean, the clouds. There is a simplicity of view, and a calming space emerges.

If you take off on a stormy day, there is that magic moment when the plane penetrates the cloud layer and the warmth of the sun pierces through the window. Not only do you have perspective on the smallness of life below, but now you have the elation of noticing what is occurring. There is no room for denial. The sun is always shining! It's the height you traverse that gives evidence to what is. This is the nature of hope. Even when we cannot see the sun, we know it's there. Maturity lives in this place. Yes, feelings and thoughts continue to ebb and flow, but the mature always know that the sun is shining above the clouds.

Someone who has never flown would not believe this to be true because they haven't experienced it for themselves. As far as they know, the sun comes, and the sun goes away. But those who have flown know the reality. The Inner Observer is your pilot and can fly you up to the sky any time you like. The minutiae of life falls away and you can see the bigger picture. The Inner Critic benefits from this perspective. When you find yourself ruminating on the situation at hand and you deteriorate into judgment, criticism, or dual thinking, get into your inner airplane, maneuver a takeoff, and rise above the clouds. Get up to where the sun is always shining and give thanks for the fresh vantage point. Take a breath there and notice how it might help you move forward in a refreshed way.

Practices for the Inner Critic

The Inner Critic is often hyperfocused. So, take two minutes to broaden and soften your gaze. If you can, go outside and look out as far as you can. Or simply look out your window and rest your eyes on the distant horizon. Take three deep breaths and let yourself expand into the space.

Write down your "Good Christian" to-do list, the practices or activities you do that you think prove your goodness. Now, don't judge it or focus on it. Simply remind yourself that these are not the main things. God is. Gently shift your attention to God and receive God's loving gaze.

Imagine yourself in an airplane taking off on a cloudy day. Picture the moment when you break through the clouds and the sun bursts through the small, oval window. How do you feel?

NOTICE, DISCERN, AND RESPOND

Notice

- Under what circumstances is the Inner Critic most likely to appear?

Discern

◉ What is it costing you to let the Inner Critic sit at the head of the table?

Respond

◉ How might you begin to craft your own pearl necklace? What is the first story you want to place on the strand?

◉ What does it look like for you to engage your Inner Observer and fly up above the cloud layer? What perspective emerges?

◉ How is God currently bringing out the best in you, developing well-formed maturity? Give thanks and enjoy this goodness.

6

From Anxious Controller
to Enjoying Life's Seasons

MOST MARRIAGES HAVE A FEW PATTERNS that get recycled over and over, with each pattern having its own kind of dance. Some dances are like a lovely waltz. Everyone is beautifully coifed and nicely dressed and the two float along the surface of the dance floor in graceful circles. However, some dances are more like the flailing that occurs in a mosh pit where the dancers push and slam into each other while frenzied music plays. I'm happy to say that after almost forty years of being together, Alan and I mostly waltz, but we are still known to engage the mosh pit now and again.

Speaking of mosh pits, Alan and I engaged in "one of those conversations" one morning quite a few years back. It began with his dip into melancholy due to the felt weight of his own angsty load. This is my "loving" and euphemistic way of describing this dynamic. I dove into my old pattern of trying to pull him up and convince him there was another way to make his way through his day. And . . . cue the mosh pit.

For most of the first half of our marriage, when Alan was depressed, I would imagine him in a deep, dark hole. I could see him sitting at the bottom of the hole with his arms wrapped around his legs and his head hanging low. This image does not work at all for an upbeat soul like me, and the voice of the Anxious Controller would take the reins. *You can't let him stay that way. This is a horrible feeling that you must remedy. Why is he feeling low? There must be something you can say that will coax him out of the hole. Let's not rest until we can figure out what to say or do to solve this.* In all my controlling glory, I would go over to the edge of the hole and yell down into it, "What are you doing down there? Come on out!" I would push and prod, but it always felt like dragging someone through a tar pit. As it turns out, my pushing was not fun for Alan either.

I'll admit, these dynamics also showed signs of enmeshment and codependency, and thanks to therapy, those tendencies have received some much-needed healing. Over time, and as we both grew in emotional health, I encountered a new image. God graciously sheds light and truth onto situations and, when I'm open and aware, I can see it. In this refreshed image, I saw Alan and I walking down a dirt road together, me on the left and he on the right. We both had our own lanes along this pathway. Occasionally, Alan's side of the road would dip down into a little valley and his part of the path would be lower than mine in elevation. Even so, we would continue walking right next to each other. At some point, he would walk uphill, and we would be on the same level path again. Because I could see the road ahead, I had a sense of journey. There were no holes and neither of us had to stop walking. This image moved my heart from the mosh pit back into the ballroom. It felt emotionally and relationally manageable.

My vision of Alan being in the hole was one of the easiest triggers in my life. Something in me would snap and I would hear the Anxious Controller. *What is he doing? He can't stay like this. Ugh. I have to do something. I must get him to leave that dank place and come back to the light.* The Anxious Controller is just as it sounds, tenaciously determined and like the demanding boss of a thankless job.

There is a stark difference between the two images, the hole and the road, and I'm happy to report that the road analogy is more often how I view Alan's dips. It is not my job to stop and pull him out. We don't have to stop walking and no one is stuck. He will lift up again at some point. We are still walking side by side, and everyone gets to be where they are and who they are. After seeing that new image, I felt lighter and more hopeful. My hope does not rest in me or in Alan. My hope rests in God alone who is indeed the guide along our paths.

THE VOICE OF THE ANXIOUS CONTROLLER

The Anxious Controller is a double whammy of inner dynamics. It begins with anxiety: *Oh no! So many things could go wrong! What if I fail? What if I look stupid? What will others think?* But then, right on the heels of this, there are layers of added energies of the need to control. *You can't lose control. You must push your way forward. You've got to be sure this goes down the way you want. You'll be safe if you manage every detail.* It isn't difficult to see how pushing, trying, or angsting emerges from this kind of thinking.

Anxiety and control easily could have been pulled apart and given their own chapters. There is plenty to say about both dynamics and voices. But I find they often work together. My anxious connection to a poorly defined threat can devolve quite rapidly into a grasp for control. I don't like feeling the blanket of anxiety about a particular person or situation, and so I move to managing and controlling as much as I possibly can. This is an illusion because the only person I can control is myself.

It is important to mention that if you have ongoing, deep-seated anxiety, it might be good to seek a counselor. Chronic, overwhelming anxiety is not something to ignore if it is prevalent and affects the quality of your life. There may be childhood trauma that needs to be addressed and some of the rewiring might require a skilled hand, especially if you have experienced severe trauma. I encourage you to seek help. You are worth the time, money, and effort it takes to seek this kind of help.

Over the course of six years, we spent thousands of dollars on counseling for both of us. I joke that we could have purchased a new car for that amount. And, yes, we could have. But instead, I ended up freed from my family of origin issues and with the gift of being an independent and more functional human who is now flourishing in the second half of life. *You are worth it* is so much more than ad copy for hair dye. The reason I was ready to hear and so quickly act on the words *stop pushing, stop trying, and stop angsting* is because a deeper inner work had already been accomplished.

It would be nice if we could protect ourselves from all anxiety-producing situations. But we know this is not possible because life consistently happens all around us. I want to live, as much as I can, from a non-anxious, calm, discerning, centered space. And yet I don't want to keep myself from trying anything new or scary for fear of being pressed beyond the calm. Sometimes, being anxious or afraid shows you are pressing yourself out beyond your edges. You are trying something new. You are growing—and this is good news. Anxiety may rise up, but it doesn't have to be our boss. We can notice it and address it with our Inner Observer.

These last few years, I have been out on my edges in almost every way vocationally. I have been anxious multiple times and, as we know from my Italy story, it pressed me beyond my ability to cope. But I am still learning and growing, and I am not allowing fear or anxiety to keep me from pursuing new dreams and goals. I have learned to catch myself more often in that space between anxiety and control. Noticing, discerning, and responding to the anxious thoughts can help calm you so that a need to over-manage doesn't follow on the heels of anxiety.

> Noticing, discerning, and responding to the anxious thoughts can help calm you so that a need to over-manage doesn't follow on the heels of anxiety.

OLIVIA'S ANXIOUS CONTROLLER

Olivia is a high energy woman in her late forties. With addiction and a wild lifestyle in her past, Olivia felt a deep need to hold it all together so as not to slide down that slope again. She was most recently the Director of Children's Ministries at a large suburban church. A large part of her identity and value was tied to this position, and she took it very seriously. So much so that she would expect her volunteers to arrive thirty minutes early for their Sunday morning shift. She would stand at the door as they arrived and glance down at her watch to let them know they were a couple of minutes late. She even created a chart where she logged everyone's entry time and she would hand out report cards showing how often they were tardy. She cringes now as she remembers her behavior from so many years ago.

In Olivia's mind the behavior of her volunteers was a direct reflection on her, and she would have no part in them detracting from the capable leader she was trying to project. If they looked good, then she looked good. Her anxiety ran high because her community was known for "putting you out" if you did something wrong. This kept her drive high for proving her value, and anxious controlling ensued. She was the answer-man. If you had a problem, she knew how to fix it. This proved overbearing on her friendships, ministry relationships, and family.

Here are some examples of Olivia's unhelpful thoughts:

I need to be in control of everything or it will get away from me.

I'm going to blow it again. I'm going to burn down my own life.

I need to look good.

I need to be valuable for what I do, not who I am.

If they know the truth about me, they will not love me. They'll get rid of me.

These unhelpful thoughts rumbled around inside Olivia's heart and head causing considerable pushing, trying, and angsting. In early marriage, and with young children, Olivia fell back into addiction. This persisted until she was stopped cold by a panic attack while standing in a Sunday school classroom. She had been secretly numbing, out of control, and beyond her own ability to regulate herself. It proved to be too much. She entered her own church's recovery program and found it to be too intense and not gentle in any way. There was no grace. She wanted to make some headway, but instead she experienced further trauma at the hand of her own community.

Olivia realized she needed to step down from ministry for a while in order to take care of herself and her family. People were shocked, as they had no idea she had a drinking problem and could not believe what they were hearing. She had been a completely functional and controlling alcoholic, and they didn't suspect a thing. Stepping down created a big shift because she no longer had a way to prove her value and worth. She no longer led or taught, and it took her six months to adjust to her new normal. Over the course of that time, she learned to let people love her up close. No longer hiding, she was revealing her true story and her real life. Olivia discovered she could be loved as the true version of herself. She didn't have to keep people at bay through work and hiding. Failure became her friend. In fact, it was failure that showed her that her controlling leadership persona was just that—a mask, and one that had become too burdensome to carry.

Olivia learned to do the daily work of simply being herself. This meant becoming comfortable with being uncomfortable. The addicted version of herself never wanted to feel uncomfortable. Over the course of time, she built up tolerance for discomfort and pain and joy began to emerge. The dailiness of being transparent with safe people helped as she shared with trusted friends who listened as she decompressed. There was no shaming or judging. Brené Brown has shared that our shame wounds occur in community, and they are healed in community.[1] Olivia experienced this as she was held by friends who didn't judge.

New helpful thoughts began to emerge:

Failure is a gift. It means I'm trying new things.

You are never good at something when you first try it. Try anyway.

I can experience the love of God.

God rescues me and his love for me never changes.

Over time, Olivia began to serve again at her church. As God has been working in her heart and life over the last few years, she finds herself growing and expanding inwardly. This growth has moved her out of that position and into one of seeking the next move of God in her life. She knows she feels called to children, writing, and encouraging, but the form of that is still taking shape. In her own words, Olivia shares:

> Without the twins of power and control running the show, I was able to unclip my wings, and do the things that God is calling me to do. The voice of God directs me. The presence of God comforts me. But more than just comfort me, it leads, spurs me on, excites me, and never holds me back. It fuels me.[2]

Olivia's journey took time. In fact, it took years. Trust was a key dynamic for her as she learned to trust God more deeply for all that she needed, and she learned to trust herself to stay on the path. For Olivia, the Anxious Controller's voice subsided as she learned to embrace failure, persistence, and God's love. She is now energized by the freedom she is experiencing. This same freedom is available to you. You may not struggle with alcohol addiction, but most of us deal with something in our lives that holds us back. How might you, like Olivia, begin or continue your journey toward freedom?

GOD'S VAST EXPANSE

At one point along my journey, I experienced an artistic paradigm shift. Prior to that, I believed abstract art was pointless. I didn't understand it at all. I saw it as just a bunch of shapes, lines, and colors with no meaning. I preferred art that spelled it out for me, understandable landscapes and portraits. I didn't completely throw out my appreciation for pedestrian art (as one artist friend labels it).

However, at that point in my journey, shape, light, color, symbolism, and mystery all felt more like home. Pat answers and everything laid out all nicely and in order felt lifeless and unhelpful. There is, of course, an order to the universe, but there is also a kind of random beauty all around us. Is there not beauty in the jagged edge of a mountain peak, the white ruffled curve of a wave breaking onto the shore, the random way branches and leaves grow on a tree? A new way opened for me, and the rigid lines in which I had colored began to fade away.

It can be tempting to look to God for explanations and answers alone. The Anxious Controller is the queen of this. She wants to manage and achieve conformity so that everything and everyone can be held in her grasp. But this kind of clutching can create a kind of "McLife" as it becomes more difficult to be open to the mystery of God's vast holiness. God's grandness precludes me from completely wrapping my mind around all of who God is. This might be a point of frustration to some, as mystery hangs over us like the mist on an early morning meadow. However, for me, there is a kind of comfort in accepting God's largeness, God's mystery. I allow myself to be surrounded by and swallowed up in God's vast expanse.

There is a natural peace that emerges when I recognize my smallness. That peace translates into freedom for the voice of the Anxious Controller. Laying down the weight of the world and becoming an appropriate size is just what the Anxious Controller needs. Deep in her heart, she wants to rest; she just doesn't feel safe enough to do so. Opening to mystery, experiencing the vastness of God's presence and love, and learning to let go of the rigidity of coloring in the lines can help the Anxious Controller soften so that your own voice can be heard.

> Laying down the weight of the world and becoming an appropriate size is just what the Anxious Controller needs.

THINK SEASONALLY

Most mornings, I walk our dog, Lex, up and down our neighborhood street. A while back, I noticed one of our neighbors was getting rid of some shrubs in front of her home. As time progressed, I saw the dirt being prepared as dark plastic went down and bark chips were spread out. Soon after, small flowering plants were arranged in two neat rows. It was lovely. However, soon after, we had an unseasonable cold snap, and more than half of the flowers wilted and died. As I walked past the dead flowers, I wondered to myself if I, like my neighbor, had ever tried to begin something new when the timing wasn't quite right.

Over the course of our lives, many of us begin to believe that things should continuously grow bigger, bolder, better, and broader. We should be ever expanding and constantly productive. This cultural pushing even ends up within our church systems—implicitly, if not explicitly. However, simply looking at the seasons of the year shows us that *there is a time for everything*. Along our formational journey, it is better to look more often for *invitations* rather than shoulds, have tos and oughts. Sometimes, we try to force something on ourselves that may not fit at the time. A better move might be to set aside some time to meet with God and listen to see if you can discover where you are in your journey. Maybe God is inviting you to something that suits exactly where you are. This is so much better than preempting God's move in your life by controlling. Each of us ebb and flow in and out of seasons physically, emotionally, spiritually, intellectually, and relationally. It would help our souls greatly to pay attention to these movements and work along with them. What if our soul had seasons, just like our planet? What might that look like?

Is it summertime? Are you basking in the sun and enjoying the pleasure of activity? Is it a time of energy and re-creating?

Is it fall? Is there a bountiful harvest in which you get to participate? Are you bringing in the fruits of your labor?

Is it winter? Are you in a deep state of rest as your branches have been pruned, with your roots going deep and the sap replenishing you from within?

Is it spring? Do you sense new life, new possibilities, new growth?

It's okay to recognize and lean into your current season. The Anxious Controller might function like that unseasonable cold snap that wilts and kills the new growth. Thinking seasonally can help calm the Anxious Controller because we are reminded to let go and expand our thinking. God meets us in different ways in these seasons. Accepting this can calm a tendency to push, try, or angst. God certainly isn't requiring a tree in winter to bear any fruit. And a tree blossoming in spring isn't thinking about pruning yet. With grace, allow yourself to be exactly where you are, and walk with God there. Welcome the *invitations* that resonate with the season in which you find yourself. When the Anxious Controller sees that you are trusting the seasons of your life, she might begin to relax into a sense of safety.

> With grace, allow yourself to be exactly where you are, and walk with God there. Welcome the *invitations* that resonate with the season in which you find yourself.

REFRAME THE SITUATION

Sometimes, working with anxiety can be as simple as reframing the situation. A friend once mentioned to me that the physical sensation of anxiety and excitement can feel the same physically— a growing sense of anticipation, an accelerated heartbeat, butter- flies in the stomach. She suggested that sometimes, when I think I am anxious, I might actually be excited. As I pondered this idea specifically in light of my public speaking anxiety, I found this to be a helpful shift. Sometimes my physical manifestations were me looking forward to what was going to occur. I simply misinter- preted the sensations. The Anxious Controller would take over and compose a narrative that sent me on a worst-case scenario journey. But if I could stop myself at the start of that and say something aloud like, "Wow. I must be excited. I can feel it. I actually am excited. Look what I get to do in the next few hours. This is amazing!" Making this shift and speaking it out loud created a new narrative of excitement and good anticipation rather than fear, dread, anxiety, and control.

Over time, the desire to share and encourage has far outweighed the anxiety of standing up in front of people. There is an unmis- takable energy that happens when you are blazing a trail, and the physical manifestation of that can be interpreted as anxiety or ex- citement. It is good to discern which it is and then either continue the journey of overcoming anxiety or lean into genuine excitement. The cherry on top of shifting from an anxiety to an excitement narrative is the reminder that I can meet God in that situation. God is *with* me in it. I am not alone. It's the feeling of being alone that exaggerates the anxiety. Excitement plus God-with-me changes the story completely.

Psalm 18:1-3 (*The Message*) reminds us that God keeps us safe.

I love you, GOD—
you make me strong.
GOD is bedrock under my feet,
the castle in which I live,
my rescuing knight.
My God—the high crag
where I run for dear life,
hiding behind the boulders,
safe in the granite hideout.
I sing to GOD, the Praise-Lofty,
and find myself safe and saved.

Anglican bishop and author Todd Hunter has said, "If it can be done with anxiety, it can be done better in peace. If it can be done by manipulation, it can be done better by honesty. If it can be done in anger, it can be done better with love."[3] Unpacking this quote could be a chapter in and of itself. But let's focus on the first phrase: "If it can be done with anxiety, it can be done better in peace." The first step is to believe this is true. What would it look like to try this on the next time you feel anxiety rise up within? You could pause and take a deep breath. Maybe you are just excited. See if you can choose peace. Rely on God, your castle, your high crag, your granite hideout. Then see what happens next.

THE OCEAN OF GOD'S LOVE

I want to leave you with a vision of being enveloped by God's love. This is a very personal image that I experienced during a time of prayer. I was able to leave all my cares in the capable hands of Jesus. I share this with you, hoping you will also be inspired to be with the one who loves tenderly and unconditionally. And I pray this image begins to calm the Anxious Controller.

I was standing on the shore of the ocean. As I looked out to the horizon, there was a golden glow where the sky met the water. I lingered on the sand as I gazed at the bright light in the distance. I began to soar swiftly out and over the ocean. As I moved farther away from the shore, I could feel the cares of my day-to-day existence fade into the background. I lost access to the weight of my worries. I flew out until I was enveloped by light, where I came to a stop. I hovered in the golden glow for a while, soaking up the warmth. It was an experience of John 8:12, "I am the light of the world. Whoever follows me will never walk in darkness, but will have the light of life."

The light melted away, and I found myself in a beautiful forest. The ground was uneven with little moss-covered mounds, rocks, tree roots, and tiny ponds of clear water. There were tall, majestic trees, just enough to feel enclosed but few enough to let the light shimmer in from above. Green leaves and pink-and-white flower petals fell from above. My daily cares were gone.

I wore a long, off-white gown with a wreath of flowers in my hair. I met with Jesus as he took my hand and sat me down next to a tree with nubbly dark brown bark. I leaned my head back and took a deep, cleansing breath. Jesus stayed near, just walking slowly across the moss. I noticed a blank journal in my lap. At first, I thought, "Cool! Now I can write down everything he says."

Jesus gently chuckled. He took the empty journal from my lap. Without words, he let me know that he would write in it himself. I noticed a little red construction paper heart. He would write directly on my heart. I didn't need my journal. Jesus continued to walk slowly near where I was resting up against the tree. I could hear no sounds, yet we were communicating. Every once in a while, I would giggle. It was a very warm and relaxing time, the fruit of which was peace, an experience of 1 Peter 5:7, "Cast all your anxiety on him because he cares for you."

The next time you are tempted to push, try, or angst, try entering into this prayer with me. Father, Son, and Spirit envelop you with light, truth, and presence. What does it feel like to stand on the shore? To soar over the water? To rest in the golden glow? What might Jesus want to write on your heart? Allowing yourself this moment of love might calm the Anxious Controller within you. There is no need to be anxious in this scenario. There is no need to control. Your cares can melt away in the light of God's loving presence.

Practices for the Anxious Controller

The next time you sense rising anxiety before an event, pause to see if you might actually be excited. If so, try to shift your inner narrative by saying something like, "Wow, I'm really excited about what's coming up next."

Spend a minute with this idea: "If it can be done with anxiety, it can be done better in peace." See if you can take yourself one level deeper into believing this is true.

Picture yourself on the ocean shore looking out to the horizon or on the top of a mountain with an expansive view. Feel the small, right-sized version of yourself. Let the weight of the world slide off your shoulders. Breathe.

NOTICE, DISCERN, AND RESPOND

Notice

◉ When does the Anxious Controller most often attempt to move to the head of the table?

Discern

◉ What is the Anxious Controller keeping you from enjoying?

Respond

◉ How do you feel pressed out beyond your edges right now?

◉ How might thinking seasonally help you gain some perspective?

◉ Which image most affects you from the ocean of God's love story? How might you linger with that image for your own healing?

7

From Complaining Victim
to Walking in Freedom

HAVING LIVED IN SOUTHERN CALIFORNIA for over thirty-five years, I have grown accustomed to two types of weather: sunny and warm, and sunny and cold. We experience a few days of rain or clouds, but most of the time it's just blue skies and sun. On the other hand, I spent my childhood in rural Washington where I experienced some very harsh winters and all four seasons. The Pacific Northwest is known for its rain, and there were a few years when we encountered unexpected showers—even on the Fourth of July. I distinctly remember this because we would hold our own fireworks show in our front yard with my dad as the master of ceremonies. It's very difficult to light a match when water is pouring from the sky.

One of the most painful winter experiences I can remember included ice rain. Imagine tiny freezing needles hitting your skin as the wind propels them toward you. It is as unpleasant as it sounds. One day, when I was in junior high school, an ice storm came through during the night and created a thick layer of ice over everything. Our car was weighted down and frozen to the ground, and our front door was glued shut by a thick wall of ice. A clear, glassy blanket had draped itself over everything in sight. It took my dad many hours to pry open our front door to attempt to free the car and get to work.

THE VOICE OF THE COMPLAINING VICTIM

This same trapped feeling is the dynamic that lies at the heart of the voice of the Complaining Victim. It is the idea of having no choice— paired with the dynamic of feeling unseen—that can trigger this voice. Circumstantial and relational issues pour down like ice rain, and soon we find ourselves imprisoned with a growing fear we may not escape. This easily devolves into blaming others and easily morphs into nagging or complaining. Even though we may be in a difficult circumstance, we can choose to believe we are not powerless. It is this shift that allows us to work through our unintentional barricade and make our way out the door.

The Complaining Victim typically emerges when we have not placed appropriate boundaries in our lives. We tirelessly put ourselves out there for others and get nothing in return. This is when the voice rises to the surface: *Why does this always happen to me? I don't have time for this. My whole day is messed up now. Nothing ever goes the way I want it to. If only they would change, things would be so much better.* We don't believe we have the power to be free of such circumstances. This is a big, fat lie. We *do* have the power and we find it in a two-letter word: *no.*

No. Such a small word. Why is it so hard to say? Guilt. Obligation. Pride. But sometimes "no" is actually "yes." Yes to margin. Yes to boundaries. Yes to rest. To what might you say "no" so that you might say a hearty "yes" to something greater? This is a key question to hold as you make your way out from under the voice of the Complaining Victim.

FIND A SOLID PLACE

I've spent many years being easily swayed by the actions and opinions of others. I was incapable of seeing myself as separate from the web others had spun around me. This was due to my own lack of healthy independence, and it easily led to the Complaining Victim. I resorted to victim mode because I had given

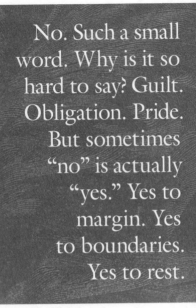

No. Such a small word. Why is it so hard to say? Guilt. Obligation. Pride. But sometimes "no" is actually "yes." Yes to margin. Yes to boundaries. Yes to rest.

control of the storyline to others and then felt my only choice was reaction mode. If only *they* would change their behavior, everything would work out for me. I didn't have a category for stepping aside, unhooking, or letting go. So, I swirled around in endless inner tirades at the mercy of the Complaining Victim.

At one point, I journaled this prayer:

God, I need you to come in, sweep out the old way and grant me a new kind of peace so that when other people are losing it, I don't lose it. Make a new solid place in me where I stand firm and don't get swayed by moods or words from anyone. May I be moved, held, stayed only by you.

This is the raw version of my prayer as I began to wake up to the unhelpful influence others were having on me. The Complaining Victim gains steam as she careens out of control. As I flap around like a flag in the wind, she has no choice but to turn up the volume on victimhood—which slides easily into complaining. That solid place within me was uncovered by finding a renewed sense of self. Part of that work was gaining a sense of individual personhood with healthy boundaries.

As I have grown in my own confidence, my assurance in God has grown as well. These dynamics are intertwined. Without a healthy sense of God's love for me, how can I make my way to the center of holy confidence? On the other side of the coin, without a healthy sense of self, I end up thinking I am unworthy of God's love, and it remains unattainable to me. This solid place I prayed for is a combination of refreshed confidence in who I am in Christ, paired with the growing assurance of God's nature and how much God loves me. These dynamics grow together and create a firm foundation on which to stand.

AMELIA'S COMPLAINING VICTIM

Amelia is a lovely woman in her early fifties who grew up in a ministry home. Her parents modeled for her a life that was overly sacrificial for the church and without healthy boundaries established. Her parents would often leave their vacation early (the only down time during the year) to go back home and attend to the needs of the congregation. It was in this boundary-less soil the seeds of over-responsibility were planted. From these seeds, unhelpful thought patterns emerged and became intertwined with Scripture which made them that much more insidious. How can you untwist a thought when there is just enough truth attached to make it seem untouchable? Her vision of a good Christian was downright biblical:

Lay down your life.

Take up your cross.

Consider others more important than yourself.

Add to that her own thoughts:

I need to come through for others.

*If someone needs help, you drop what you are doing and you go
help them.*

Don't expect people to give to you.

You are not the one who receives, you are the one who gives.

Out-of-context truth is quite dangerous, and it can become a
recipe for burnout. "Lay down your life" and "take up your cross"
are surely invitations of Jesus. And so are "remain in me," "my yoke
is easy," "my burden is light," and "my peace I give you." It is the
combination of these passages that give us a picture of a whole,
integrated life.

Twisted truth was the hammer, and Amelia's self-confidence was
the nail, as she continued to suffer the blows. This was evident in
her early life, and she took this way of thinking into her marriage.
She spent years in the wake of her husband's extramarital affair and
ever-increasing narcissistic manifestations trying to be the "good
Christian wife." This meant continued bending and acquiescing
to all of the same unhelpful thoughts. Give—and give more—
without expecting anything in return. It's not a surprise that the
Complaining Victim arose. She was beaten down and the pre-
vailing dynamic was a sense of utter powerlessness as more unhelpful thoughts emerged:

This is as good as it gets.

There is nothing I can do to change this.

You need to tough it out.

You need to be content with crumbs.

Lower your expectations.

When she tried to come out from under these thoughts with
behaviors in her life, she was often labeled as demanding or

controlling. This continued until her body finally cried out with a loud, "No more!" She contracted mononucleosis that lasted for three years, and it was immediately followed up with a diagnosis of chronic fatigue syndrome that lasted another ten years. Her body shut down and would no longer allow her to live the way she had been living, which was largely boundary-less, over productive, and over responsible. She no longer had any bootstraps to pull up.

It was during this physical shut down that she discovered the spiritual practice of solitude and silence. This was her great "waker-upper" and she found herself reading, listening, and learning. She engaged a counselor and a spiritual director as she discovered soul care and self-care. Daily, she lived the reality of Psalm 23: "He makes me lie down in green pastures, he leads me beside quiet waters." There was a shift in her marriage and family life as others began to pick up the slack. Over time, she and her husband tried to make another go of it with counseling, but his narcissism and the specter of his affair proved to be too much. Their marriage ended in divorce.

Along the way, two people offered some input that helped shape her growth. As she described some of her dysfunctional, boundary-less relationships, a counselor once said, "Yes, they are doing this, but you are getting something from this as well." At first, she didn't understand how she was complicit in the weight of these relationships. But after some inner searching, she found she was gaining a false self of self-protection. She had a great fear of being abandoned, being disliked, and having others think poorly of her or being angry with her. Unconsciously, she determined that if she kept up her end of the dysfunction, she got to feel "safe." Because of her counselor's observation, Amelia was now awake and could begin noticing her part. This began her journey of independence.

Later, in her business, as she was trying to get it off the ground and become financially viable, a friend piped in, "You know, you are your own worst enemy." Amelia was never charging enough and was making decisions based on heart rather than financial need. There was no balance of the two. This tapped into her tendency to please. This new idea of being her own worst enemy propelled her to begin to make decisions for her business which, in turn, benefited her family. But it also aided her own soul and growth. She had taken another step back from enmeshment. She was standing on her own two feet and making wise business decisions.

Amelia is now on another path. She is no longer a slave to unhelpful thoughts and more often engages her new way of thinking and living. Along the way, she began to realize the people pleasing that enflamed the Complaining Victim was *her* issue and was not about others. She awoke to this in stages over the course of her life. Her new thought was, "If I'm allowing this, then I can change it." She became more capable of pushing back when necessary and not getting steamrolled. Her growing confidence began to quell the Complaining Victim.

As for the way Scripture became twisted early on, she learned to respond to the invitations of Jesus and the relationality of their connection. No longer about rules, she enjoys relaxing into the good and beautiful relationship offered by a loving Trinity. This took some unlearning as well, but she no longer feels trapped by half-truths attempting to keep her in line.

Amelia was determined to value herself and she built on that over time. The biggest insight for her was that she was not responsible for other people's feelings and actions. Even in stressful or uncomfortable situations, she became more capable of remaining separate from others, so the lines weren't so blurred. Everyone gets to make their own decisions, and she doesn't take unnecessary blame for their feelings. All of this quells the Complaining Victim because Amelia is no longer feeling trapped. She is more confident and has a healthy sense of self. The thick blanket of ice-glass melted, and she is capable of moving freely within her relationships and responsibilities.

LOOK WITHIN

One of the ways the Complaining Victim remains active is we continue to believe we are defenseless or incapable. *If only* is one of the victim's favorite phrases. If only she . . . if only they . . . if only it were different. The *if only* is typically pointed outward rather than inward. It is so much easier to deflect and look outward for the change to occur. This is a difficult pattern to change, but it is not impossible. It first takes courage to look within and ask a few questions. What is causing me to blame others? What is at the root of my resistance to looking inside myself for help and direction? How might I access the courage I need to change this pattern?

Once we learn to look within, see what is there, and embrace our own voice, we no longer need to react to the Complaining Victim's whims. We can practice asking for what we want. The hard part is we may not know what we want because we haven't yet taken the time to listen to our own desires, wants, and hopes. It is not selfish to know what you want to do and then do it. Healthy independence is the key to all our relationships and, yes, it's an inside job first. In the process, we continue to ride on twin rails: receiving the boundless love of God as well as extending love and care to ourselves.

This can feel "easier said than done," especially if you have experienced capital "T" trauma such as sexual, physical, or emotional abuse. These are very real forms of pain, and there are times in our lives when we are, in fact, helpless and defenseless. My heart goes out to you as you journey toward healing. Many of the ideas in this chapter may not seem feasible because you have deep wounds that need tending first. This journey can be long and arduous in the wake of capital "T" trauma because we might wonder where God was as we suffered at the hands of such evil intentions. It is important to have a trusted counselor as you plumb the depths of your pain. If you are currently in a dangerous or abusive situation, this is not the time to quell the voice of the Complaining Victim. Please reach out for help and get safe.[1]

YOU ARE NOT TRAPPED

The Complaining Victim tends to keep us attached to our circumstances rather than differentiated and secure. One of my mentors is suffering from an increasingly debilitating physical condition and her body is undergoing severe changes. The medication she is on sometimes affects her mental capacity. She moves slower and things just take longer. She is making the adjustment with great grace, and I learn from her as I watch her adjust to her body's new reality.

One day, at a café, as I poked at my breakfast hash browns, we were discussing her health. She surprised me when she said, "I'm okay. My body is doing other things, but *I'm okay.*" The way she stopped, looked me in the eye, and asked for my attention showed me that she was talking about her deepest self. Her *self* was okay. *Who she is* was okay.

Those two words threw me into a paradigm shift. *I'm okay.*

Her body is falling apart and yet she truly and deeply knows that *she*, her inner person, is okay. This helped me learn to gain a bit of distance from my circumstances, feelings, moods, preferences, and expectations. I had been letting my circumstances and moods *define* me. No matter what is going on around me—or even in me—I can be okay in my deepest self. Nothing else defines or determines how I am. Suddenly, Scripture began to flood into my mind:

I have been given everything for life and godliness (2 Peter 1:3). I'm okay.

I am fearfully and wonderfully made (Psalm 139). I'm okay.

The Lord is my Shepherd. I have everything I need (Psalm 23). I'm okay.

The eternal God is your refuge, and underneath are the everlasting arms (Deuteronomy 33:27). I'm okay.

The deepest and most real part of me, in Christ, is okay. Circumstances may belie this, but existentially it is true. Situations around me may not be perfect, but I am not defined by that. This is not to be confused with the dynamic of the Positive Thinker. We are not going into denial here and glossing over real loss or tragedy. We are talking about seeing things as they are, just like my mentor, and still knowing, way deep inside, I'm okay. Psalm 62:6 puts it this way, "I will not be shaken." In fact, what my mentor shared with me about herself is a direct reflection of her belief in these words: *Yes, my soul, find rest in God; my hope comes from him. Truly he is my rock and my salvation; he is my fortress, I will not be shaken* (Psalm 62:5-6).

> No matter what is going on around me—or even in me—I can be okay in my deepest self.

The Complaining Victim wants to keep you imprisoned, undifferentiated. "You are trapped, and you cannot escape!" she proclaims. But she is wrong. You are not trapped. In the core of your being, you are okay. You are more than okay. You are a beloved daughter of a God who is your rock and fortress. This is unchanged by circumstance. "Outwardly we are wasting away, yet inwardly we are being renewed day by day" (2 Corinthians 4:16). This is the truth.

My mentor had no idea that her words touched me so deeply. It is her great suffering that brought her to the place of differentiating between her *self* and her physical state. I am still learning how to walk this out, and I am grateful she shared it with me.

LIVE EXPANSIVELY

A few questions emerge in this quest to listen to our inner voice and manage our inner narratives: *Who do you want to be?* And here's the follow up question: *What does it take to get there?* What you do now is a part of who you will become in the future. You can begin by asking: *Who am I already?* Not on the surface, but deep down inside, the formed, crafted, loved me. What is the essence of my truest self? This would be a wonderful journal exercise or something to ponder in prayer. Continue to be open and then make small decisions every day that release the old and invite the new. Worry, fear, and stress are not the boss of you. Put them in the back seat and take the wheel of your life.

What will it take to become a woman who knows who she is and is unafraid to boldly express her God-given voice and abilities?

Dear, dear Corinthians, I can't tell you how much I long for you to enter this wide-open, spacious life. We didn't fence you in. The smallness you feel comes from within you. Your lives aren't small, but you're living them in a small way. I'm speaking as plainly as I can and with great affection. Open up your lives. Live openly and expansively. (2 Corinthians 6:11-13 *The Message*)

> What will it take to become a woman who knows who she is and is unafraid to boldly express her God-given voice and abilities?

Even though the context of this passage is that of conflict with others, it might not be a stretch to use it in our case here where we might be in conflict with ourselves. Wherever in your life you feel small, please do not remain stuck there. This is a glorious invitation to live freely. The Complaining Victim often creates unwanted barriers. Open your life. Engage the freedom that is yours and live expansively.

CONSIDER THE BIRDS

Complaining occurs naturally when gratitude wanes. It's easy to see, point out, and dwell on the negative. In fact, our brains are wired for negativity bias. Brain scans show our brains react more intensely to negative images.[2] This is, in part, due to the innate need to be kept out of harm's way. It is built-in self-protection. However, just because our brains react in this way, doesn't mean that we need to remain in that narrative. We aren't very often being chased by a bear, but sometimes we find ourselves in that mode in the regular situations of our lives. By pulling out our Inner Observer and taking one step back, we can remember this bias and choose a different way forward. Fortunately, Scripture so often guides us toward good and helpful thinking.

Jesus encourages us to look at the flowers and the birds and how they are cared for. Matthew 6:26 says, "Look at the birds of the air;

they do not sow or reap or store away in barns, and yet your heavenly Father feeds them. Are you not much more valuable than they?" God has set up this earth so that birds have all they need to survive. They can find food and all the materials they need for nesting. They've been given instincts to mate, care for their young, and keep themselves safe from predators. If that much effort has gone into birds, how much more has been given to me? There are many ways we are encouraged to be transformed by the renewing of our minds. What we focus on can determine our moods, emotions, and our actions.

As often as possible, try to take in the care of God in all its varying forms. We are bombarded with the unhelpful and the unholy every day. It takes effort to swim upstream against that current. A little gratitude, wonder, and awe may help the Complaining Victim take her place at the table. And, as with all the voices, be sure to thank her in the process. The Complaining Victim kept you awake to the fact that something was off-kilter and needed to be looked at. This is a great gift. Thank her and let her know you'll be on the lookout now, and that you'll use your new-found confidence to be sure you are not taken advantage of.

STAND IN YOUR OWN SPACE

The Diving Bell and the Butterfly[3] is one of the best movies I almost didn't watch. The trailer piqued my curiosity, and I was drawn to the idea of the story. The movie is a biopic about the life of Jean-Dominique Bauby, former editor of *Elle* magazine. Bauby suffers a devastating stroke and loses all function except for his left eye and his mind. For the remainder of his life, he lives with locked-in syndrome.

At first, the story is almost unbearable to watch as the director chose to show it from a first-person perspective. We are looking out of Bauby's one functioning eye. Blurry images move strangely around him, and he finally realizes that he can't move, and no one can hear him, but he has full brain function. The voice he is speaking with is merely his thoughts, and we are the only ones privy to them.

At one point, the doctor determines that Bauby's eye is not functioning properly, and the treatment is to sew the eye shut. Again, it shows the scene from the point of view of looking out that eye. Stitches are sewn until the screen goes black. He begs them to stop, but the medical team, of course, cannot hear, and so they keep sewing. It is a terrible, claustrophobic sensation. The director of the film did an impeccable job of helping us to feel with the protagonist.

The miracle and saving grace of the story is a speech therapist who works with Bauby in the horribly tedious exercise of communicating with him. Using a letter board, with common letters shown first, she speaks the alphabet and when he hears the letter he wants, he blinks once with his one good eye. She proceeds to write down his words, one letter at a time. In fact, they became so good at this method that he even wrote a book using it.

Throughout the movie, the image of the diving bell recurs. Bauby is in an old-fashioned diving suit made of metal with the big round helmet and glass face piece. Like the ice that blanketed our home, it is a similar symbol of him feeling heavy, weighted, and trapped. For the first part of the movie, we experience life from the protagonist's point of view. Finally, there is a turning point where he decides to stop living in self-pity. Here is his inner monologue as he makes this inner shift:

> I've decided to stop self-pitying myself. Other than my eye, two things aren't paralyzed. My imagination and my memory. They're the only two ways I can escape from my diving bell. I

can imagine anything, anybody, anywhere. . . . I can imagine anything I want.[4]

At this point, the movie transitions to third person and we begin to see Bauby from the outside. The sense of being trapped is now relieved, and his world is enlarged. I will admit, this is an unusual and exaggerated story. But when the Complaining Victim is in charge, we may experience the same sensations of the diving bell—feeling weighted, sinking slowly into the depths, and trapped in the land of no choices.

At some point, like Bauby, we might grow weary of the weight, move through it, and come out with a new, stronger sense of self. Walking through the devastation, he acknowledges what he lost and then decides to focus on what he can control—his imagination, his thoughts. If you are burdened by the thoughts of the Complaining Victim, now is the time to remember that you do not control other people or situations, and yet you do have access to the fruit of the Spirit of self-control. You get to choose your yeses and your noes and how you will proceed.

I often worry about things that don't matter, and I sometimes don't enjoy what I have. My invitation, in this case, is to open my eyes wide and see. The simplicity of waking up each morning, the full use of my healthy body, loved ones and friends who are trustworthy and available; these are all gifts from our loving holy community—Father, Son, and Spirit. The Complaining Victim doesn't take the time to ponder any of this. She creates grumpy narratives about the past or the future, neither of which we can change.

Rather than pushing, trying, or angsting, return to the solid place, that holy combination of assurance of God's love and your own enlivened confidence in yourself. Stand firmly in your own space, and you won't feel the need to play the victim. As we let go of the past and future, the weight of the unchangeable and the unknown begin to fade. The thick blanket of ice begins to melt, and freedom becomes available right here and right now. This is how you remain on the path toward wholeness.

Practices for the Complaining Victim

Take a moment to go outside or look out a window. Notice the birds or some nearby flowers blooming. Rest in their presence. The birds are cared for and so are you. Sink a bit further into this reality.

Get out a piece of paper and list some simple pleasures in your life. Dynamics that exist right now. Be in the present moment and consider your five senses or your innate giftedness. Look at the list and enjoy it.

Borrow my raw journaled prayer and make it your own:

God, I need you to come in, sweep out the old way and grant me a new kind of peace so that when other people are losing it, I don't lose it. Make a new solid place in me where I stand firm and don't get swayed by moods or words from anyone. May I be moved, held, stayed only by you. I need healthy blinders.

NOTICE, DISCERN, AND RESPOND

Notice

- How might the Complaining Victim arrive on the scene when you're having an off day?

Discern

- What is making it difficult for you to let go of the dynamics of the Complaining Victim?

Respond

- How does "if only" keep you from making your way forward? How might you look within for strength?

- Knowing that our brains are wired for negativity bias, how might you intentionally embrace more helpful thoughts?

- Choose one of the four previously mentioned "I'm okay" Scripture phrases. How does it inspire you? How might it breathe life into you today?

8

From Passive Spectator to Inspiring Through Presence

SURROUNDED BY TALL PINES, desert wildflowers, and warm dry air, I made my way up into the mountains to help facilitate a retreat. One of the speakers that week was a man who taught with fire and eloquence. He was truly a gifted teacher. The content of his teaching, however, turned out to be a bit polarizing. So much so that one of the female leaders in the room was in tears as she described, in the moment, how his teaching made her feel as though she had no value. Another female leader was so angry she couldn't speak; she simply seethed. It was truly uncomfortable.

The next day, because I had a role of oversight in the event, and because he was likely going to continue teaching in the future, I shared with the man that I didn't think what he said was appropriate for our formational tone and process. It wasn't so much the content; it was more the *manner* in which he shared. It was neither conducive to nor similar to the retreat vibe we were trying to foster. This led to some bold and honest words on both our parts. We didn't hold back and yet we parted amicably with a hug and an affirmation of our friendship.

About a week later, we found ourselves at another conference, and we decided to touch base about our previous conversation. As we were talking about his teaching material, he let me know that his ideal audience was young male leaders. No problem there. Everyone gets to choose who they are, what they say, and who they say it to. But then he made a comment about not wanting to talk to fifty-year-old women. His statement had an unintentional tone of condescension. Holding back my steam, I don't remember exactly what I said, but I know I addressed the comment in real time. No one's mind was changed, and we both heard each other. Again, we parted ways, with our friendship intact. However, that one phrase stuck in my craw, and I was unable to shake it for some time. *I don't want to talk to fifty-year-old women.* I know I took it personally because I had recently turned fifty. It also stuck with me because I had my own issues I hadn't yet dealt with, and this moved them to the surface.

The North American culture in which I live tends to discount people as they get older. In many ways, we worship youth and what is new and fresh. Just take a look at any beauty product ad and you will see that we are being trained to believe that looking and being young is best. Who on earth would want a wrinkle, thin lips, a sagging chin, or a sunspot? Not when there's Botox, fillers, or the latest creams. These anti-aging issues in our culture can cause many women to feel as if they are being pushed out from the center of things. This is tragic because women hold us together in so many ways over the entire course of their lifetime. The women over fifty who I talk with are just hitting their stride. They are looking for ways to contribute based on all of the life wisdom they have gathered up. This is actually the time for their voices to be heard and their teachings to be embraced. They have the wisdom, and they have the time. And even though I believe all of that, I still had to look myself squarely in the eye and admit that I struggled to embrace other aging women, which meant that I was struggling to embrace my own aging. The conversation with this young male leader brought all of this up to the surface. *Fun.*

At the heart of this situation was my own self-acceptance. Could I embrace my own aging process? Could I love my body? Could I accept my age? Could I lead from this place? These were the issues. And they became a part of the fire that continued to move me from Passive Spectator to Bold Proclaimer. In so many ways, my fifties have been about hitting my stride, and the interaction with that man was evidence of my having moved out beyond the voice of the Passive Spectator. In the old days, I would not have said anything. I would have simmered on the sidelines, complained to my husband, and over time, this incident would have become a distant memory. Instead, this was a moment for me to speak out. What happened in that room was not appropriate, and I was the only representative leader in there who could speak to what occurred. This was a part of my own process of peeling away from the wallpaper and moving into the room.

> The women over fifty who I talk with are just hitting their stride. They are looking for ways to contribute based on all of the life wisdom they have gathered up. This is actually the time for their voices to be heard and their teachings to be embraced.

Because of the courage I engaged in that situation, my self-acceptance has increased as has my passion for coaching and training women. As I learned to embrace myself, and my age, my heart for women of all ages enlarged. I had to jump over the hurdle of valuing myself, and others like me, enough to spend the time pouring into myself and then them. I long to empower the next generation of women who will come forth to lead in their families, workplaces, and communities as well as women in the second half of life who are pouring out their wisdom in all their glory.

I share this story as one way to illustrate how I moved through the Passive Spectator dynamic in my own life. Even though I had been a leader in one capacity or another since I was nineteen, there was always a voice inside of me that wanted to keep me small, to defer, to hold back. Over the course of my life, I would enjoy breakthroughs in this area, but embracing my own aging and reinforcing the value of women over fifty was a major breakthrough, and it has become a freight train of energy I enjoy to this day.

THE VOICE OF THE PASSIVE SPECTATOR

At first glance, the Passive Spectator doesn't seem to be a problem. She presents as low key and quiet, staying out of everyone's way. However, not far under the surface, low self-worth, self-doubt, or fear of making waves can perpetuate some unwelcome dynamics. *I'm sure it will work out. I wouldn't want to rock the boat. I don't know enough to speak into this. My opinion doesn't matter anyway. Someone else will step up. I don't want to put myself out there.* This voice is just as unhelpful as the others because she keeps us from moving forward in any number of ways.

Sometimes, it seems easier to blend in with the wallpaper or to live vicariously through others. But neither of these modes leads to the joy of finding your own voice, speaking up, and moving forward with confidence. Other times, we remain passive because we are overwhelmed. It's not that we don't care, it's that we care so much that it all becomes a big pile we can't see beyond. This leads to a kind of shutting down as the Passive Spectator calms us with the idea of taking a back seat. *This is too much. Let someone else do it. What could I do about it anyway?* The sidelines become a place of safety. Rather than determining what we want, creating healthy boundaries, and advancing, it is sometimes simply easier to fade into the background.

SOPHIA'S PASSIVE SPECTATOR

Sophia is a vibrant woman, wife, mother, and grandmother. For years, she taught eighth grade and has been involved in some form of ministry for most of her life. Growing up in a ministry family, she was well versed in serving in the church. However, the Passive Spectator has long had the microphone and ran the show for most of the first half of her life.

Outwardly, Sophia came across as confident, accepting, accommodating, and at peace. Yet inwardly, she was bound up, avoidant, and asleep to her own longings, wants, and preferences. She felt inwardly oppressed and struggled to find her voice. So much so that she didn't even really have a category for the search. She was willing to give up mutuality in relationships just to have friends. This meant she was willing to do most of the work, making for lopsided connections. For Sophia, the Passive Spectator offered quite a few thoughts leading to the inner oppression she described:

Think about what others want.
Don't explore what you think, feel, or want.
Don't dream.
You don't know your own thoughts.
Your voice can't make a difference.
Please others—even if you must go against your own conscience.

Value how others perceive you.

Be quiet.

These thoughts worked for her . . . until they didn't. Over time, she found herself embarking on a new journey of finding her voice. Sophia challenged her long-held thoughts and beliefs and she came to find that, in Christ, there are options. She began to see that God was honoring her heart and her voice. She learned to know God's posture and voice toward her, and she decided to please God rather than focus on other people's preferences.

Sophia experienced one of these shifts during a time of prayer as she sought Jesus' guidance in this area. One striking image that moved her along this path was that of an open window. She imagined herself standing inside a home in front of a second-story open window. The cool, God-given breeze was blowing in and brought refreshment to her soul. This fresh air carried with it a sense of joy. It was welcome and life-giving. However, at times, the window would suddenly shut. God's presence seemed to vanish, as the air in the room became stale, almost suffocating, and she couldn't figure out what triggered it. So, in prayer, Sophia decided to ask Jesus why this was happening. She discovered that it had to do with her tendency to get stuck inside her own head. Like a leaf trapped in an eddy of a winding stream, she was no longer in flow. The closed window jarred her awake to this, and she realized she had a choice. She could move out of that enclosed room. Her invitation was to enjoy a more wide-open space. Once she understood this, she experienced a great deal of consolation.

Back in the image, making a discerned decision, she moved down the stairs of the home and out the front door. From the driveway, she gazed back toward the house. She was surprised to notice Jesus joining her there in the front yard. He put his arm around her and said, "We can talk about this whenever you want to." Sophia felt this as an honoring of her own voice and choice to engage this process. She experienced freedom in being known and by having her voice invited. She moved away from the old way of thinking: *Why would God want my voice or thoughts on anything? What do I have to offer?* Rather, she felt invited by God the Father and by Jesus to speak her thoughts, feelings, and desires. This potent image, as well as other deep inner work, has moved her further into her own expansive space.

Sophia is now overcoming the angst of the Passive Spectator in three primary ways. First, she will often ask God in prayer, "What do you think of me?" This question brings her to presence and returns her to a loving, gentle, beloved posture as she remembers who she is. Second, she sees her life with God as an invitation. She is co-laboring with God and not carrying everything alone. Third, she continues to practice a rhythm of life. She has patterns of practices and engagements that are unique to her, and she finds solace in keeping these rhythms.

A big part of Sophia's journey toward finding her voice was that she didn't go it alone. She invited people into her story. Her husband and a few close friends would hold space for her to share along the way, and she looked to them for support and discernment. Good, solid friendships are important as we engage all the parts of the journey of life. Sophia now lives more honestly with others. She says "no" more often, taking the time she needs to offer the response that works best for her. She is living more expressive of her desires as she declares what she wants and needs. In addition, she shares from a more loving, inner space and is more patient with herself. Having spent many years in this transition, she is now receiving training to become a spiritual director and is dreaming of her future to come.

Making our way to greater freedom takes time. And, as you can see from Sophia's story, there are many facets to the growth process:

prayer, overcoming angst, sharing with trusted friends, changing our view of how God interacts with us, and plenty of time. We can follow Sophia's example by being consistently proactive in overcoming our avoidant behavior. We can thank our Passive Spectator for doing her best to protect us and help her relax as we move forward with greater confidence.

TAKING COMMAND

I have kept a dream journal for almost thirty years because I've long been intrigued by what my subconscious processes as I sleep. Most of the time, it is simply housekeeping, sweeping my mind clean or working through some unprocessed emotions. However, sometimes a dream will stand out, and I take the time to write it down. Recurring dreams are especially interesting as an idea continues to knock on the door and clamor to be seen.

In my forties, I encountered a particularly fascinating recurring dream. The dream took place in the exact office space where I had spent about five years working in the corporate world when I was in my twenties. It was similar to the feeling of other common recurring dreams about going back to school but you haven't been to class all semester and you can't find your books or the classroom. In the dream, I had been absent from work for years and had suddenly returned to the office. My boss never seemed to care as we just picked back up from where we were when I left. Sometimes he was there and sometimes he wasn't, but I always had the sense that I had missed out on a great deal. I would wander around the office space, trying to get my bearings, always wondering why my boss wasn't concerned about my absence. This dream recurred for years.

However, once I transitioned from my former job into my work at Unhurried Living, the dream began to shift. When I would find myself back to work at the office, there was a new, female boss. She was tall, capable, and skillfully led the team. I only had this version of the dream a few times, but I was quite intrigued by the appearance of this new boss. The biggest shift of all came when, one night, I dreamed that I entered the office with a newfound confidence. I was so sure of myself that I initiated a conversation with the female boss letting her know that I would now be taking over. I was ready, capable, and I would be leading the team from now on. She quickly agreed and I became the boss. I was running the show.

Of course, there may be more than one way to interpret these dreams. You can clearly see a bit of the heroine's journey in there, as well as a woman who is aiming at the empty nest and looking out into the future in a new way. However, I'd like to talk about my dream in terms of the Passive Spectator. The movement from employee to boss is striking. At first, I was a long absent employee trying to figure out how to enter back into my work, always hesitant, always concerned about what the boss would think. Still passive. Over time, as I continued the journey of finding my voice in all the various ways, my subconscious was beginning to show me the progress I had made. Not only did the boss shift from male to female, but I made the huge leap in asserting that I was ready to be the boss of the office. The Passive Spectator was no longer running the show when it came to my work. I was out in front and embracing it.

The Passive Spectator wants to keep you small. She has no intention of taking risks or putting herself out there. That is why it is good to notice her voice and decide whether or not you want her calling the shots. The Passive Spectator attempts to keep us safe by pulling back so that we won't risk failure which often leads to embarrassment or shame. As with all the voices, this is not an enemy tactic. All our parts are trying to help us in one way or another. So, as always, a gracious and loving stance can help us out here. As we've done with other voices, we can thank the Passive Spectator for her help and allow her to take a rest at the dining table. Assure her that you are growing and capable of taking more decisive action that suits where you are right now.

Once she has quieted, you might find yourself experiencing the fruit of greater confidence. Notice over time these subtle shifts in your energies. Where in your life, right now, do you sense a new-found energy to take command? Not in a domineering way, of course, but in a graciously bold and confident way. Grant yourself some space to see where the leading edges are for you right now. Then take the risk to move out there in just one small and simple way.

I KNOW WHAT I'M TALKING ABOUT

Another way I learned to quell the Passive Spectator was to grow in the confidence that I do, in fact, know what I am talking about. Most of us deal with self-doubt over the course of our lives. For a long time, I didn't trust my own thoughts, feelings, or gut reactions. Whether it was a fact or an intuition, I tended to doubt or second guess myself. All my adult life, I have been a curious and voracious learner. Yes, I have a degree and a handful of certifications, but on top of that I am an autodidact, and I take my own personal and spiritual growth and development seriously. Deep questions become deep prayers, and I hold space for God to show me what lies under the surface of the issues. I collect my findings in my heart as well as my journal.

Over time, as I would read formational authors I respected or listen to gifted speakers, I would hear them say things that I had already learned from the school of life. These weren't puff-me-up moments. Rather, they were clarifying. I remember thinking with a hint of surprise, *if other authorities are saying these things too, then*

I must know what I'm talking about. What I had learned through trial and error, the school of hard knocks, and prayer was also written by a respected author or shared in a sermon or other training. What I really learned was that wisdom and insight is given to all who ask, seek, and knock. God is quite generous that way. I was learning to be confident in the wisdom I had gathered and sharing it without hesitation or apology.

As time progressed, I began to turn this clarity into inner trust. Rather than being afraid to share what I knew for fear of being wrong, I trusted that what I shared was valid and even helpful. Slowly, but surely, I began to grow in confidence when I spoke to others. But the deepest change occurred inwardly. The Passive Spectator was quieting. Her usual *just stay in the background* or *don't make waves* or *let's keep hiding* mantras began to fade. I began to awaken to the fact that I knew what I was talking about. I learned to trust my own knowledge, wisdom, competence, and gifts. Self-doubt still arises from time to time, but it no longer holds me back.

> Give yourself permission to speak up and act on your wisdom, and let that courage build on itself over time.

Learning to trust yourself takes time and it is an important aspect of owning your own space. Give yourself permission to speak up and act on your wisdom, and let that courage build on itself over time. The Passive Spectator then takes her seat next to an open and confident woman.

PRESENT WITH QUALITY

I've never really considered myself a writer. I simply and deeply desire to share what I know, and writing is one beautiful way to do that. Over the years, I engaged various blogs as I continued to pour out my latest musings. Not because I wanted to write, but because I wanted to encourage and inspire. A few years ago, this longing to inspire began to deepen and the desire to engage writing in a more formal way emerged. I wanted to launch another blog, but this time with a focus on women. I longed to pour out my heart in ways I hadn't before. The dream was humming along nicely until I was stopped by this thought: I cannot begin without knowing my writing voice. This did not stop me before, but this time it felt like I was creating something even more meaningful, and I wanted it to be my best. I was certain I needed to have my voice identified and determined before I could begin. It was on a beach walk with a dear friend when I discovered that I had it backward.

I remember saying to my friend, "I don't want to begin blogging until I know what my *thing* is." This was my awkward way of describing my writing voice. I began with the theme of "presence" but there was this elusive "thing" that I was chasing. When I read other bloggers, I knew what I was getting because I was accustomed to their voice, the things they shared and the way they shared them. As we continued to talk and as my friend asked helpful and insightful questions, I realized you can't find your writing voice prior to writing. You must write to *discover* your voice. My voice emerged naturally from the *act* of writing. This seems obvious now, but, at the time, it was an epiphany for me.

A refreshed passion for the new blog came to the forefront, and I felt a new surge of creativity and ideas. I spent the next year, along with a few other friends, producing a blog for women. I took many of the most important things I had learned, experienced, and journaled over my lifetime, and I turned them into blog posts. Each one felt like a small child, like something I had birthed, because I was giving voice to that which was inside of me. This was when my more current writing voice emerged.

In my struggle, you can see another way the Passive Spectator can keep us stuck. *You have to know what you are doing first. You can't just go out there and do it. You have to know what your voice is. Take more time to discover it before you put yourself out there.* The Passive Spectator loves bargaining for more time. But sometimes the exact opposite is true. You must speak, write, share, or act to find out who you are and what you are about. Your voice emerges from actions, even if they are imperfect. My writing style emerged one blog post at a time, until my writing voice was evident, and I could see it clearly.

This is not simply about writing. This is about life. Your unique voice emerges as you practice using it in whatever form suits you. It can be as simple as your day-to-day conversations. Taking risks to share what you really think without care about the judgments of others. Moving out from behind fear or laziness and acting on that new project of yours. Putting it out there a little at a time or in one fell swoop. And all of this is done imperfectly and that's okay. What matters is that you take the risk and try. Determine to move from Passive Spectator to Glorious Sharer! Trust me, the world needs whatever the authentic version of you produces.

According to author Macrina Weidekehr,

> Everything in life can be nourishing. Everything can bless us, but we've got to be there for the blessing to occur. Being present with quality is a decision we are invited to make each day. . . . There is nothing so healing in all the world as real presence. Our real presence can feed the ache for God in others.[1]

Pushing, trying, and angsting jolt us out of presence and this is when the Passive Spectator can insert herself. We can overcome this voice by being "present with quality" as Weidekehr states. No longer held back by fear or apathy, the freedom here is quantitative as well as qualitative. For the sake of others, we step out of ourselves and share fully. This is our motivation and calling.

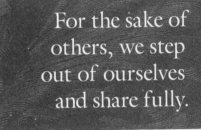

For the sake of others, we step out of ourselves and share fully.

My encouragement is this: don't wait until you think you are ready to begin. Begin imperfectly. Engage presence and let your true voice emerge. Don't let the Passive Spectator win out as she tries to twist, turn, confuse, and keep you small. *Find* your voice by *using* your voice and let yourself soar.

Practices for the Passive Spectator

Is there a situation in your life in which it would be healthy to speak up for yourself or on behalf of someone else? Consider what you might say and how you might say it. When you are ready, plan to speak up. Then speak.

Journal at least five things you know are true about yourself or about life itself. Then read back through the list and let some confidence emerge.

What could you begin to engage that enlivens your voice? It could be anything: writing, dancing, speaking, painting, jogging, and more. Choose something that energizes you and begin to engage with intention.

NOTICE, DISCERN, AND RESPOND

Notice

◉ What causes the Passive Spectator to surface on any given day?

Discern

◉ What is the price you pay when the Passive Spectator is running the show?

Respond

◉ How have you struggled with self-doubt and your own value or worth?

◉ What would it look like for you to become the "boss" of your own life in an increasing way?

◉ In what area are you holding back until you "find your voice." How might you step forward and move toward discovery in action?

9

From Unsettled Heart
to Being at Home

As I walked out the front door and down the concrete steps, I had no idea I was about to stumble on to one of my deepest aches. As we do quite often, Alan and I were setting out on one of our "walk and talks" within our neighborhood. I had no thought or intention to plunge my depths. And yet, there I was, with cars whizzing past, weeping from my gut on the sidewalk of a suburban street.

It began as a good old-fashioned rant about our house. I do this every once in a while, to let off some steam. I process my disgruntled thoughts about the state of our forty-year-old house, and Alan listens while I drone on. At the time, we had been living in our home for almost twenty years. We rent and the upgrades to the structure of our home fall to our landlord; therefore, major improvements simply do not receive attention. I will admit that my unhappy speech sounded quite petty and complaining. I was aware of this and yet I still found myself in a swirl of discontent. Our house is stuck in the 1970s with all of the original doors, aluminum windows, and Formica countertops. I railed on and on and grieved the loss of not having a dream home that I made my own.

I was really going for it while Alan patiently listened. I had warned him that I just needed to process to get it off my chest, and he was the gracious recipient of my "spewage." I was on a roll when, suddenly, a sentence came out of my mouth that stopped me cold. I barely got the last word out as I lost my breath and felt a sob get stuck in my chest.

I don't have a home.

Most people are unaware that I was adopted as a newborn. And this issue of not having a felt bodily bloodline, a kind of home, has come up for me before. For many who are adopted, there is an underlying sense of a missing piece that hums along quietly way deep down inside. This does nothing to negate my actual family in which I was raised. There is, however, a unique dynamic of being formed in one womb and then raised by heart and hands not attached to that womb. This is a conversation that could be a book in and of itself. But, in my case, it's enough to say that there was a preverbal dynamic that lingered from this passing from one mother to another.

Years before this walk and talk, I had worked through my adoption at many levels in both counseling and spiritual direction. But the phrase, *I don't have a home,* came from that inner space that still feels the sting of that missing piece. It pointed directly to the true nature of my issue about our house. Rather than merely being about the structure in which we live, it was about my searching for home at my deepest level.

THE VOICE OF THE UNSETTLED HEART

The voice of the Unsettled Heart often has its roots tethered to a real and deep desire. There is nothing wrong with our desires and longings. And there is nothing wrong with expressing ourselves from our hearts. We can notice our desires, and name and engage them. I want to be sure you understand the dynamic we are talking about here. In no way am I saying that desires and longings are bad and we should try to suppress or quiet them. It's exactly the opposite. We must get in touch with our truest longings and our deepest desires. These are God-given and are the key to becoming more authentically us, inwardly and outwardly. It's when longings remain unseen, untethered, or hopeless that they can devolve into being unsettled, which keeps us at arm's length from contentment.

It's less preferable having the *unaddressed* and *overly pessimistic* Unsettled Heart acting as our boss. Especially when it manifests as a low-lying dark cloud of hopelessness that we can't seem to see past. *I'll never have what I need. I'll never be who I truly am. This will never work out. Something is missing. I don't know what it is, and I'm not sure I can find it. I feel incomplete and this search never seems to end.* It's rough going if these thoughts are consistently sitting at the head of your inner dining table or leading the way. They lack healthy energy and even a modicum of hope. Sure, doubts and uncertainty arise for all of us, and can even grow our faith, but parking here in an endless cycle can keep us stalled. We can engage our longings and connect them to hope, while paying attention to the Unsettled Heart and thanking her for her help.

The Unsettled Heart keeps us connected to our wants and desires

> We must get in touch with our truest longings and our deepest desires. These are God-given and are the key to becoming more authentically us.

—and this is important. However, somewhere along the way there may have been a grievous loss or betrayal. So, it makes sense that this voice might turn inward. If she runs the show, we can fall into a melancholic hole from which it is difficult to exit. Left unattended, and at the mercy of pushing, trying, and angsting, the Unsettled Heart can keep us restless, disheartened, or unsatisfied.

CHARLOTTE'S UNSETTLED HEART

Wearing a sailor dress and Keds, with her hair pulled back in a ponytail, eleven-year-old Charlotte was running through the door from her house to the garage ready to find her ball. She stopped suddenly when she noticed her dad backing out of the garage. Normally, this would be a mundane moment on any regular day. However, Charlotte could see furniture and clothing piled high behind her father in his car. He gave no explanation. He didn't say goodbye or I love you. He simply glanced at her and drove away. Confusion, sadness, fear, and questions jumbled up inside her little body. The combination led to her emotionally shutting down. She made an unconscious decision to not feel. Her longings and desires were locked away, and the key would elude her for many years. It was too much, and no one was there to help her process. In the trauma of her own loss, her mother overdosed on valium and was unable to support her in her grief and confusion.

As an adult, Charlotte would pour herself out caring for others in their time of need. So much so that she would sometimes end up ill herself. She then berated herself with negative self-talk: *What's wrong with you? Why are you weak? Why can't you fix this? You worried so much you made yourself sick.* A litany of blame and shame ensued until she finally stumbled on to a dynamic within her. She was trusting God in most areas of her life except when it was about her personally. This went back to that early belief that her feelings didn't matter and therefore *she* didn't matter. She wasn't important enough for someone to walk her through the process of her dad leaving, so, in her little mind, she just didn't matter. And she *longed* to matter. Enter the voice of the Unsettled Heart.

Over the course of her life, these were the thoughts with which she struggled:

Why bother risking any conflict by speaking my thoughts and feelings because no one really cares?

I'm not going to tell anyone my desires and dreams because they don't matter to others.

People value me for what I do; therefore, I need to work hard to be valuable.

When I'm working and serving others I matter. When I'm not, I don't.

Can you see her underlying desires within these thoughts? It is a desire to be seen, cared for, and valued. These desires are beautiful and valid, and yet, wounded and undiscerned, it kept a large part of her hidden. Charlotte's basic belief was that it was better to deny herself than to risk conflict. This led to producing for acknowledgment. Many years later, while praying, she encountered Jesus' encouragement for her: *Charlotte, I didn't die on the cross so you could work for me.* Striving to be worthy was pervasive in her life, and this realization was halting. She was awake to how the denial of herself kept the Unsettled Heart alive: *I don't have what I need. I must earn it. God will take care of me when I'm worth it. But when I'm not, and I'm weak, then I must be all alone. My feelings don't matter. I'm not important.* There is no confident resolve in these words of the Unsettled Heart. These thoughts left a gaping wound

in her heart, and she had lost touch with the truth that she was
God's beloved.

A lingering question emerged in a conversation with a spiritual
director: "Charlotte, why do you have so much trouble showing
compassion to yourself when you can show it to everybody else?"
She realized she was afraid of being stuck as a victim. She had seen
this in others and didn't want any part of that. Her spiritual director pointed out that she was already, in fact, a victim. At eleven
years old, she was the victim of neglect, emotional abandonment,
and more. All her inner work had been good and helpful, and yet
it didn't negate the needs she had as a child. She had made her way
to forgiveness and compassion toward her parents as an adult, and
yet the wounds were still lingering. She realized that if she couldn't
trust Jesus himself to have compassion on her, then she was, in fact,
stuck in the very way she was trying to avoid.

Her entire adult life, Charlotte had longed to feel like someone's
priority and never felt that was the case. She was awakened to the
idea that she could prioritize herself. Not in a selfish way, but in a
healthy "love others as you love yourself" way. We do have a part in
meeting our own longed-for needs. If she couldn't make herself a
priority to herself, how could she become a priority to anyone else?
She found solace in asking God to search her heart. She wanted to
be free from the ways she was unaware of these inner dynamics that
kept her stuck. She had what she coined an "Oz" moment. She realized that all she had to do was click her own heels together in the
form of compassion on herself and she would be transported home.
Rather than denying feelings and remaining stuck, the longings of
her heart could be seen by not only God, but by herself.

Charlotte may have tried to avoid conflict, but that kept her from
living the story of her life. Conflict and risk are difficult but worth it.

She had also learned the memories that formed those ideas came through the understanding of an eleven-year-old little girl. The important thing for her was to go back and meet with her inner child. To acknowledge her feelings and then allow her adult self to feel the feelings in the present, to continue the process of healing. The compassion she began to have for herself spilled over into compassion and forgiveness for others. It was a loving fruit of her process. She met her Unsettled Heart by facing the difficult aspects of her own life.

The Unsettled Heart can be a masterful guide into our pain and past trauma. It is important to follow the leading of this voice in order to plumb our depths. And we can learn not to become trapped under the weight of this voice's heaviness. For many of us, this might require the help of a professional, depending on the severity of the wound or trauma. Like Charlotte, we can sometimes bury our desires until the Unsettled Heart rises up and clamors to be heard. In this way, the Unsettled Heart is a gift. Therefore, we don't judge, despise, or dismiss any of these voices. We learn to notice, discern, and respond to them so that we can integrate, heal, and become more whole.

> We don't judge, despise, or dismiss any of these voices. We learn to notice, discern, and respond to them so that we can integrate, heal, and become more whole.

STREAMS IN THE WASTELAND

The message for the Unsettled Heart is this: God sees you, knows you, and can meet you within your deep desires. God provides and will, ultimately, make your way. "See, I am doing a new thing! Now it springs up; do you not perceive it? I am making a way in the wilderness and streams in the wasteland" (Isaiah 43:19). The Unsettled Heart can feel like that dry, cracked ground with no hope of replenishment. Me trying to satisfy myself is like pouring a glass of water onto the sand and believing a creek will be formed. It is God who provides streams in the wasteland. The stream occurs *in* the wasteland, and a way is made *in* the desert. Our terrain may not change, but in that very place a new thing can occur, and living water can refresh even the driest place. The invitation is to hold this mystery and remain open to the available hope.

I once visited a landscape nursery and noticed a section of plants arranged on tiered shelves. Above the stack of plants was a worn wooden sign painted with the words, "Drought Tolerant." "These plants must be tough," I thought to myself. They can withstand the heat and the absence of needed water. The Unsettled Heart can be transformed as it learns to hold on with hope as it waits for the stream.

Sometimes the Unsettled Heart simply needs a gentle nudge in the right direction. The Unsettled Heart might make its way forward with these new thoughts: *Today, I will lay down my tendency to believe that I will remain unfulfilled. I will act as if grace abounds because it does. I will create without limits, without categorizing, without making any promises about the outcome. I will act as if God loves me exactly as I am and looks fondly toward me with great affection.* God's grace is present, and love flows tenderly in the direction of the Unsettled Heart like a stream in the desert.

> God's grace is present, and love flows tenderly in the direction of the Unsettled Heart like a stream in the desert.

MOVE THROUGH NEUTRAL

Because the Unsettled Heart tends to feel its deficits more than its abundance, moving toward hope might seem more than a little daunting. Our circumstances may be difficult, and the struggles may seem unending, but we do still have a say regarding our thoughts about them. We decide what to plant in our heart and how that gets expressed through our lives, even amid difficulties. This is the plot for any great biography, people who persevered with grace inside of, and despite, their difficulties. We can be people who take the time to address our thoughts about our situation so we can continue to express the fullness of who we are.

The Unsettled Heart might be reluctant to move toward optimism or hope because it seems too large a mountain to climb. Trying to move too quickly to a more helpful thought may be too big a move for lasting change. When moving from an unhelpful thought to a more helpful, hopeful thought, try stopping off at neutral and intermediate thoughts first. It's not as big a leap. You could then make your way from neutral to more descriptive statements that you can still affirm.[1] There is no rush here. You can stay at the neutral and intermediate thoughts as long as you need to, even if it is weeks or months. Linger with them until you believe them, and the original unhelpful voice begins to fade. Body issues hit close to home for most women, so let's try this idea with thoughts about our bodies. One thought progression might look like this:

I have an ugly body. (unhelpful thought)

I have a body. (neutral thought)

My body is God-given, and God is an artist who creates beauty. (grounding truth)

I have a beautiful body. (helpful thought)

Take your time with this. Move to the neutral thought and stay with it as long as you need to. Once you can say that sentence with integrity, move to the grounding truth and stay with that until you are ready to move on to your new helpful thought. As always, be gracious. Self-flagellation doesn't do any good and it can cause us to loop or to become stuck. Simply stop, notice, and graciously turn. If you catch yourself thinking and believing the old thought, simply notice and pivot to your new neutral or grounding thought.

This type of self-awareness is the same dynamic we find in contemplative prayer. In contemplative prayer, you set aside a number of minutes to simply be silent in God's presence with no agenda. Of course, during that time your mind flutters and wanders; however, you will have chosen a prayer word that you can quietly speak that brings you back to presence. Words such as love, Jesus, God, here, or now. You utter the word to gently pivot yourself back into your space. That same gentle movement can be accessed as you make the change from an unhelpful thought to a more helpful, gracious thought. A gentle, unrushed, step-at-a-time approach makes for more lasting change.

I DO HAVE A HOME

During most of my forties, I held onto a kind of fantasy. I called it a hopeful dream and desire, but in many ways, it was still a fantasy. I longed for a mansion that we could use as a suburban retreat center for people needing that kind of space in Orange County, California. In this part of the country, home prices are outlandishly expensive, and yet I spent hours and days dreaming about this space, what it would be like, what ministry would occur within its walls. I was even able to get a couple of realtors to show us some homes in the hopes we could raise funding for such a retreat. But the funding never emerged, and the dream was never fulfilled. Over the years, I came to be embarrassed about holding onto this impossible dream. *What a waste of time*, I thought. *How naive and unrealistic.*

During that same time period, I had recurring nighttime dreams about a huge home with many rooms. Every time I would visit this mansion, I wanted it to be mine, but it always belonged to someone else. Sometimes the home belonged to another strong and capable woman, and I could never figure out how to make the home my own. I would wander the home and continually find more rooms and areas I didn't know about. It went on and on, and I never really saw the entire structure in any dream. There was always more to discover.

In Jungian terms, each part of a dream is an aspect of yourself. So, in my case, the mansion was me and, in that season of life, I was continually longing for and uncovering large spaces deep within. New spaces for myself and others to enjoy. The strong women in my dreams were also me. It was just a version of myself that I wasn't fully in touch with yet. I hadn't quite grown into her. It took many years, but, in my dreams, I did become the owner of that home. Externally I was looking for something that was dynamically occurring internally, but it would be many years until I would notice the transformation.

Fast forward to a few years ago, well past the memories of the dream mansion. I was enjoying worship singing on a typical Sunday morning at church. My thoughts flashed to the mansion that I held as a fantasy for those many years as well as the recurring dreams of the larger-than-life home. The Spirit whispered this thought, *the home you wanted is you.* At that current time in my life, I was experiencing the beauty of that large, spacious, and expansive place. As a spiritual director and coach, I engaged often in spiritual hospitality. That longed for place was my own heart.

I have become that mansion as I hold space for women to share, to be heard, and to explore God and themselves. And I have a never-ending vision for the expanse of that God-given space. This brings me full circle back to the sidewalk as I cried, "I don't have a home." At the time, it felt so deeply true. But, God, in his faithfulness, took all the various parts of my story and brought them together in one glorious chorus, "The home is you." Added to this is the beautiful knowledge that God dwells with me and in me. It's not just my home, it's our home.

How many ways are there for God to show himself in a woman's life? Endless! What I saw as a frustrating number of unknown rooms was actually a wide-open door to possibility. Not knowing where it ends is part of the grace of the expansiveness of God. God formed me over all those years so that his temple—me—became the place I longed for. Holding the dream home idea (that I thought was a fantasy) was not a waste.

It is me.

And it is you.

Yes, you are an ever-growing, spacious home. Your home may look different from mine and it may serve a different purpose, but it is large, expansive, and you can take the time to explore and dream. Don't ever believe you are done expanding. So much more awaits no matter your age or season of life. The Unsettled Heart wants you to think you will never be satisfied or fulfilled and that simply is not true.

Perhaps the Unsettled Heart can find a bit of solace in Psalm 63:1-5:

> You, God, are my God, earnestly I seek you; I thirst for you, my whole being longs for you, in a dry and parched land where there is no water. I have seen you in the sanctuary and beheld your power and your glory. Because your love is better

than life, my lips will glorify you. I will praise you as long as I live, and in your name I will lift up my hands. I will be fully satisfied as with the richest of foods; with singing lips my mouth will praise you.

Here we see that we are truly satisfied when we take our thirsts and longings to God. David, the psalmist, acknowledges he is surrounded by dry and parched land. He is not in denial, and he embraces his longings as they move him toward God. He reminds himself what is true of the past, present, and future. And he declares his satisfaction in God. So don't be afraid of your longings. Harness the depths of them. They lead to your own healing which is a beautiful movement for you and can shine a light on the path for others.

Practices for the Unsettled Heart

The voice of the Unsettled Heart is tender and can help you connect with your desires. Take a moment to acknowledge this part of yourself. Let her know that you will pay greater attention and you will care for her. Notice your feelings as you make this connection.

What is one thing you can say aloud right now that is true about God or yourself, even if you have an inner sensation that something is missing?

Practice taking one of your unhelpful thoughts and moving it through neutral to helpful. Stay on the neutral and grounding thoughts as long as you need until you are ready to move on.

NOTICE, DISCERN, AND RESPOND

Notice

- When does the Unsettled Heart usually present itself in your life?

Discern

- What makes it hard for you to embrace the Unsettled Heart?

Respond

- How might you get more in touch with your deepest longings?

- What area of your life feels the most parched? How might God be providing a stream in the wasteland for you?

- Envision your own expansive inner home. What rooms are waiting to be explored? What gifts might be expressed within that space?

10

Engaging God's Voice

OUR THOUGHTS ARE LIKE Post-it notes we carry around in our pockets. We walk around labeling everything we see, beginning with ourselves. *Too fat, too thin, too loud, too quiet, too much, not enough.* Post-it after Post-it, we categorize, classify, and catalog. It's exhausting because we believe the words on our Post-its have the final say when, in fact, they are simply our thoughts. Our actions stem from our thoughts and emotions about our circumstances—and we wonder why we experience the results we do. Our freedom begins to emerge when we realize we are not our thoughts, we *have* thoughts and we get to notice, discern, and respond to them rather than react. Working with our thoughts and narratives is about reading those Post-its, questioning whether they are helpful or not, and then moving to wise action.

God is transforming us, and we can practice cooperating with this process. We get to be who we are and love from the center of that place. We don't control people or circumstances. We notice, acknowledge, and accept (not necessarily condone) what is occurring and, by the fruit of the Spirit of self-control, we make decisions about what we will think and what we will do.

We take in so much information every day, all day, and it can be overwhelming. As you have made your way through this book, I do hope that you will bias toward absorption, practice, and encounter. Please don't settle for mere knowledge. The invitation here is to move at the pace of grace and grow at the pace of transformation. This pace is different from the pace of question/answer or action/reaction. The pace of transformation is alive, and it relies on our cooperative responses to the invitations of God. I'll be the first to admit, this is a messy and winding process. No one gets it right the first time or even the second. Life will continue to hand us lemons from time to time, and we will experience all the ups and downs. And yet, it is possible to grow in our ability to allow our truest self to lead.

> The pace of transformation is alive, and it depends on our cooperative responses to the invitations of God.

HOW THE VOICES RELATE TO ONE ANOTHER

This is a great place to pause and talk about how all our various voices might be interacting with one another. There are never clean, straight lines in any of our processes, and this one is no different. Wouldn't it be great if our thoughts all spoke one at a time, in order, so we could easily Notice, Discern, and Respond our way forward?

For example, my own Unsettled Heart was likely being masked or pushed away by any number of voices. The Positive Thinker might have tried to push my Unsettled Heart down with thoughts like, *Let's not look at that now, that's no fun. That's too much pain to wade through. You don't want to do that.* Or my Anxious Controller or Stressed Achiever might have tried to keep me moving and in a flurry so that I didn't have time to look in the shadowy recesses of my heart. My Inner Critic might have launched criticisms that kept the Unsettled Heart at bay. These voices make attempts to keep me from accessing parts of me that need attention.

What every one of these voices really needs is love and attention. This is why learning to pause and notice is so important. Noticing is a gentle way to look within and see who has taken a seat at the head of the table. Remaining aware of your inner dynamics—while not stressing about this very process—can help on so many levels.

HONESTY AND TRANSFORMATION

Remember not to see these voices as villains that disturb our peace. All of them thought they were helping us make our way. And now they can be a part of us becoming awake and aware. Ideally, we can thank each of these loyal soldiers for bringing to our attention some needed grace in our lives. It is good to never despise any part of ourselves because, in each season, we did the best we knew how at the time. Any number of these voices got us as far as they could, and they worked until they didn't. Even if they led you down a less than desirable path, it is not too late to make the changes that lead to less pressure, less anxiety, and less overwhelm.

Something that might hinder us from moving forward here is the fear of looking at our "stuff." Many of us have spent much of our lives in appearance management mode. We have skillfully hidden the aspects of ourselves that are unseemly, untidy, and unruly. *I've packed those away nicely in a room and I don't plan on opening the door, thank you very much. Why would I want to open that up?* And, yes, that's one way to go about this. But I'd like to offer another way. A way that leads to wholeness.

The more honest and willing you are to look at your stuff, the more transformation is possible. How much do you want to grow and heal? How much freedom do you long for? Match that with deep levels of transparency, authenticity, and truth. We make our way to deeper levels one stairstep at a time. Move to the next level of honesty you can muster. Learn to love authenticity more than you love self-protection. Let your frustration with your current situation persuade you to take the risk of opening to deeper, hidden aspects of yourself. Honesty is your friend, and it opens the door for further growth. And remember: small, simple, and gracious steps are the way to stay on the humble path of transformation.

> Imagine yourself as a portable sanctuary. Your own body is your prayer room and can be accessed at any time to enter this processing space.

As we move on from here, continue to remember that you already have what you need. Imagine yourself as a portable sanctuary. Your own body is your prayer room and can be accessed at any time to enter this processing space. Simply remain open, aware, and willing as you move through your everyday life. You are the temple of God, and this temple is with you wherever you go.

ENJOYING MY GOD-GIVEN VOICE

"Finding my voice" is one way to describe coming into one's own. This is a process that took a lot of time for me. And you are likely experiencing your own version of this right now. Once I turned the corner in finding and listening to my own God-given voice, I discovered new freedoms and quicker access to two beautiful dynamics.

First, I had an overarching *shift of focus.* I became more concerned with who I am in Christ and what I am offering than what I look like, act like, and what other people think about that. There comes a time when we must stop caring what others think and embrace who we are in all our glory. We need not continue a pattern of stumbling over the expectations, criticisms, or opinions of others. Let's live the abundant life we've been given.

Second, I enjoy a more *holy confidence.* Rather than work being a clunky drudgery, I enjoy being in flow much of the time. I am experiencing an overflow of sorts, God in me and then through me. I am who I am, in a grace-filled, focused, "for the sake of others" kind of way. My inner work is ongoing, and I continue to engage my own healing process. Many fears and anxieties have fallen away, and there is now a new level of "I am who God has made me." I am enjoying myself and my life. It's not forced. It's not put on. It bubbles up and flows out.

To say there is an easy 1-2-3 method to activating my God-given voice would be horribly misleading. I simply want to share what I learned as I looked back on my own journey. Here are a few more dynamics that helped me progress.

Agree with God. Begin by remembering and agreeing with God's assessment of you. You are fearfully and wonderfully made. God knows the number of hairs on your head and catches all your tears. God is a loving father and a nurturing mother. The grace we extend to others comes more easily when we are gracious with ourselves. Conversely, we often spew out onto others that which is inside of us. Engage the difficult yet rewarding work of treating yourself with grace. Rather than being a victim of the Anxious Controller, the Inner Critic, or the Stressed Achiever, become accustomed to receiving God's voice of love and care.

Take it in and breathe deeply. Holy. Dearly loved. Friend of Jesus. Righteous. Delightful.

Live a with-God life. It is not an exaggeration to say that my connection with God has been the central through line of my life. Yes, I've lived a regular life like everyone: work, family, relationships, and responsibilities. But all of it has been in relation to what God is doing *in* me. The circumstances of our lives are not separate from the work of God within. Every relationship or circumstance has the capacity to be a learning lab. Learn what it means to connect your inner and outer lives and you are well on your way to a life of transformation.

Seek inner healing. We've heard it said that it takes a village to raise a child. Well, it also takes a village to bring healing to your inner child and all these voices. Gather wise counsel around you: soul friends, a spiritual director, a coach, a counselor. Engage the inner work of deep healing and talk about what is happening in your life. Be seen and heard by an empathetic, caring, and wise person. Be okay with the level of healing you need and seek help to find it. Scrimp and save anywhere else in your budget, but not when it comes to your own soul care and mental health. Don't run away when it gets hard. Press in and go to the depths. The freedom that is available is unbelievable.

As you make your way into your depths for healing, inner freedom is unlocked like a heavy, rusted padlock at the end of thick chains. As the first padlock is opened, a surprising process begins. All of the other padlocks along the chain have a chance to open in succession. Depending on your readiness, this can happen quickly, or it may take some time. There is no right way or right timing for this. As the padlocks open you can see with more clarity and less shame or guilt. Fear and anxiety reduce in volume. Yes, it is difficult to face our inner depths and yet the fruit is freedom from the inside out. This is the golden secret to finding your God-given voice. It's actually already there, it simply gets buried or we lose track of it. Whatever we can do to unearth what is already there is a beautiful part of our transformative process.

Get physical. This is a touchy one. I know. I have spent the last few years growing accustomed to my body that is now in its fifties. Crêpe paper eyelids, the crease on my neck, the wrinkles on my hands, a never-ending tug of war with belly fat. I only mention this because our culture pushes so hard against all of this. Youth is worshiped, and we see images of women who have tightened, lifted, and injected, all in the name of beauty. Body image is an entire subject all on its own. For now, let's talk about getting in touch with your body through exercise. Whatever means of exercise suits you, do it. Our bodies are our temples, and they are not to be ignored or despised. Let this be a part of loving yourself. It may be one of the highest hills you have to climb, but that doesn't mean you shouldn't try.

Early on, for me, it was Zumba. I would go to the YMCA to shimmy and salsa with a room full of women of all shapes, sizes, and ages. And I'll tell you this little secret: I never felt more connected to my body than when I was in my Zumba class. The sheer physicality of it all, the loud music, the endorphins, and the energy of the other women—it was so healing and empowering. I don't know what form of movement works for you, but go ahead and search it out. Then revel in the way you feel while you do it. Let it energize you. Let yourself feel connected and alive. Let the God-given endorphins help to build inner confidence which will, in turn, empower your voice.

Open to creativity. Photography became a very important creative outlet. It entered my life and did double duty as I was finding my voice. First, it was something that only I did. It didn't involve my husband or my kids. It was just me. I always wanted to learn photography, and so I taught myself how to use a real camera and I even made money for a while as a photographer. The individual aspect of it was deeply healing.

Second, photography taught me presence and how to see. I was experiencing what I can only describe as a dark night in my life when I first picked up my camera. Nothing made sense, and I didn't have useful words for myself or others. So, I just carried my camera around and took in the world through that little viewfinder. In all my silence and solitude times, it was just me, my camera, and God. Connecting with this creative aspect of myself helped me engage with God in a new way. And I am still benefiting from the fruit of that dark, quiet, and special time.

Dance. Sing. Paint. Knit. Garden. Do whatever makes you feel like you are creating. Connect your head to your heart through your hands.[1] Let God's creative nature manifest itself in you and burst forth.

Say thank you. Over time, I learned to receive encouragement as I stopped deflecting and I started listening. When someone paid me a compliment, I took it in and said, "Thank you." Believe people when they pay you a compliment. Receive it, place it in a special place in your heart, and move forward from there. It is not arrogant or selfish. It is receiving a gift. And it is good for your soul. At times, I would engage further conversation as I asked the person to describe more fully what they saw in me. And then I chose to send it inward and let it become part of me. As you let encouragement from others build up inside of you, your confidence can soar, and your God-given voice can emerge.

Finally, all of this is cyclical and seasonal. You may be humming along nicely in one area while another is sitting dormant like a tree in winter. Springtime will come for that dynamic as well. The point is to keep your own ongoing process in mind. Do what you can—when you can. And be open, aware, and willing to that which God is inviting you. What it looks like on the outside may be different for each one of us. The key is to stay on this journey. Remain aware and awake.

My story is not prescriptive of the way things will unfold for you. It is merely the way it unfolded for me. My encouragement to you is that you wholeheartedly engage the transforming process in which God is guiding you. If you keep this at the center of your thinking, feeling, and doing, you will indeed make your way toward wholeness. The world needs transformed people now more than ever.

ENGAGING GOD'S VOICE

As much as this book is about thoughts, voices, and the stories we craft, I'm hoping you'll see that all of this is held together at its core by love and the voice of God. Notice the words I received inside the Florence Cathedral were not merely *stop pushing, stop trying, stop angsting*. The first part of the invitation was *this is my body, given for you*. Jesus, by the Spirit, was reminding me of an ultimate reality. It was the intimate image of the Last Supper hanging as a backdrop. Jesus breaking bread with his friends, sharing with them the most important things he said to them up to that point. Jesus offers ultimate love and sacrifice on my behalf and yours. Love is for all of us, and it is the center of our transformation. The amount of thought work we engage is to be matched with equal effort by the determination to open to the voice and love of God in all its fullness.

In my own life, the process of this openness was kick-started when I was introduced to the spiritual practice of solitude and silence. It is in these set-aside times to be receptive to God that I learned to *listen* and *receive*. As you grow in this, a new aspect opens up inside of you and it continues to expand over time. This is the place where Notice, Discern, and Respond find their true home—your own expanded soul. If you try nothing else, please make space and time for receptivity in God's presence. Even just one hour a month will begin the expansion.

As we examine all the various voices, we'll see that at the center of each one is a cry to be seen, known, and loved. And what we find is that we already are. We simply forget to remember. Thomas Merton puts it this way:

> In prayer we discover what we already have. You start from where you are and deepen what you already have, and you realize you are already there. We already have everything, but we don't know it and don't experience it. Everything has been given to us in Christ. All we need is to experience what we already possess.[2]

Maybe life has taken its toll and the idea of our being loved unconditionally has been beaten out of us. Hurtful, wounding, or traumatic relationships and even our own self-talk can take the microphone and what rings in our ears is that true love isn't possible. And yet, we are reminded: *You already have what you need.* Use your precious time and energy to uncover that which you already have. The voice of Jesus reminds us every time we have ears to hear. Let's become more open as we engage the loving voices of the Father, Son, and Spirit.

THE LOVING VOICE OF GOD

Let's begin with the loving voice of the Father. If you have some lingering father issues and thinking of God this way makes this difficult for you, consider embracing the idea of God as mother or as, simply, God. The aspect of God we desire to connect with here is that of *creative life-giver, nurturing parent.*

The voice of God will always come through with love. At its center, even if it's corrective, will be the tone of someone who cares deeply about your well-being. The Bible contains many references to God as a loving, motherly, nurturing presence.[3] God is big enough, cares about you personally, and can hold you in whatever space you find yourself. Don't let your yet-to-be-healed parts keep you from receiving this portion of love.

If you are hearing an inner voice that is disparaging, critical, or guilt-producing, it is not the voice of God. God is forming us, certainly, but God relates to us with kindness and not shame (Romans 2:4).

God loves you. For real. There is nothing that holds back God's love (Romans 8:38-39). Not even your unfelt sense of it. Take a breath and rest in this love right now. This love can bolster your intentions to make progress in managing your thoughts and narratives.

THE GRACIOUS VOICE OF JESUS

When it comes to the gracious voice of Jesus you can simply read any Gospel story and see how he treats each and every needy and wounded person who crosses his path. From the woman caught in adultery, to the bleeding woman, to the woman at the well, Jesus consistently spoke grace. Jesus always saw the women holistically and reached toward them at all levels. He knew how to address body, soul, spirit, emotions, and relationships with a single sentence. This has always meant so much to me because it adds to my ability to receive the connection that Jesus offers.

Every Sunday, our Anglican church service culminates in the Lord's Supper (Eucharist), a most appropriate focus of every week. The table is set, the wine is poured, the bread is laid out. I walk forward, receive the bread and cup, and then sit back down in my seat. I then watch as each member of our community receives Communion, and the babies are blessed. I feel as though I share in each person's blessing as they make their way through the line. This is the weekly liturgy with my church community. There is a simplicity, a rootedness, a sweet and peaceful spirit that pervades our worship. It is Jesus, himself, saying, "This is my body, given for you."

As you engage the voice of Jesus, remember that it will come to you full of grace and truth. You will likely sense that Jesus' voice meets you on many levels at once. He's so good at seeing and embracing you as a whole person, dearly loved. Receive his grace now.

THE CONNECTING VOICE OF THE HOLY SPIRIT

It has been said that the Holy Spirit is the manifestation of the love between the Father and the Son. Their love is so potent and powerful that it is actually a person—the third person of the Trinity. This is a voice and a love that I want to open to more and more.

"And I will ask the Father, and he will give you another advocate to help you and be with you forever. . . . But the Advocate, the Holy Spirit, whom the Father will send in my name, will teach you all things and will remind you of everything I have said to you" (John 14:16, 26). Jesus said these words to his disciples in John 14. In John 15, Jesus shares one of the most important ideas of all with his followers: "I am the vine; you are the branches. If you remain in me and I in you, you will bear much fruit; apart from me you can do nothing" (John 15:5). In that same passage, Jesus also called them his friends.

This is what the Spirit reminds us: we are deeply connected to the grace of Jesus by the fellowship of the Spirit. There is no separation. Jesus uses the language of "in." You can't get closer than that. Dig in deep and receive the realities of what is being offered. Love, up close, and real.

The Spirit is a connector. The "fellowship of the Holy Spirit" is a blessing found in the New Testament. So, when listening for the voice of the Spirit, keep an ear open for an undertone of loving togetherness. Father, Son, and Spirit always humbly pointing to one another in love, grace, and connectedness. These are the colors of the voice of God.

REFLECT ON YOUR LIFE

In his book *Here and Now*, Henri Nouwen states,

> It is remarkable how much of our life is lived without reflection on its meaning. It is not surprising that so many people are busy but bored! They have many things to do and are always running to get them done, but beneath the hectic activity they often wonder if anything is truly happening. A life that is not reflected upon eventually loses its meaning and becomes boring. We have to keep asking ourselves: 'What does it all mean? What is God trying to tell us? How are we called to live in the midst of all this?' Without such questions our lives become numb and flat.[4]

Asking questions, and not primarily seeking answers, can lead to the greatest transformation. It's holding and living the questions that makes way for change. And a big part of this holding is the process of *reflection*. One of my favorite Dallas Willard quotes is, "All [the church] needs to fulfill Christ's purposes on earth is the quality of life he makes real in the life of his disciples."[5] The quality of our lives matter and our own engagement and reflection on our lives has a real and lasting effect on us and our relationships. Uncovering God's voice as well as our own God-given voice from within the pile of other voices is a meaningful way to become a person of reflection. The pattern of action and reflection is what creates a meaningful story, and it is what creates a meaningful life. We aren't just improving ourselves for the sake of ourselves. It is for the sake of others. Many of us skip the crucial work of our own becoming. This "quality of life" Willard speaks of is not merely about our external behavior. It's about *who we are* when we do what we do.

> The pattern of action and reflection is what creates a meaningful story, and it is what creates a meaningful life.

STEP INTO YOUR LIFE

For many years, there has been a little dove nest tucked into the eaves of our patio cover. Each year, a dove couple comes and turns last season's nest into their new home. A while back, one of the doves was in the nest and the other was walking around our yard looking for the perfect stick. I watched as the dove picked one up . . . too stiff . . . nope. Picked up another . . . a little bendy and soft . . . perfect. It flew back up to the nest, dropped it in, and engaged further in the search.

As the dove continued looking for the perfect nesting material, I glanced at my yard. It was a little haggard from a recent storm. Half-green, patchy winter grass. Bark chips that needed a new layer. Old, pockmarked concrete. And yet my yard had all the makings for a soft, suitable home for a family of doves. This reminds me to look deeper for the inherent beauty around me. You never know what might be hiding right before your eyes.

The lifelong journey of transformation can seem daunting at best and distressing at worst. We collect so much baggage over the course of our lives we wonder if we'll ever make our way through it all. However, among the rubble, there are hidden treasures like the ones found in my backyard by the doves. One such treasure is this: I *get* to change. I don't have to remain stuck. And I have all the time in the world to make my way toward greater wholeness. Remember, it's the pace of grace we're moving at, not the pace of the clock. We can choose a life of expectant grace. Even though life and change are difficult, we can lighten our own load a bit by remembering that we are on a transformational journey that ends in our good. It culminates in love.

> We don't yet see things clearly. We're squinting in a fog, peering through a mist. But it won't be long before the weather clears and the sun shines bright! We'll see it all then, see it all as clearly as God sees us, knowing him directly just as he knows us! But for right now, until that completeness, we have three things to do to lead us toward that consummation: Trust steadily in God, hope unswervingly, love extravagantly. And the best of the three is love. (1 Corinthians 13:12-13 *The Message*)

Finding and using your God-given voice is not about becoming brash and swinging your words and your will around like an unwieldy sword. It is about knowing who you are, growing into that, and standing firm in your own space. It is about being sturdy enough to stand in that space when everyone else around you is standing in theirs. You do not have to bend, break, or acquiesce.

You also do not have to beat anyone down or push anyone away. You can simply stand in your space, speak your mind, and be who you are, with a heart full of grace and love.

It is the long hard work of finding and using your God-given voice that grows you into the space where you can stand in confidence and humility at the same time. Do not be afraid of the journey that you must go on as you make your way to wholeness. It is not selfish. You are a beloved child of a redeeming God, and it is okay to act as such. Humility is not thinking *less* of yourself. It is thinking *rightly* of yourself. You are fearfully and wonderfully made. You will never be loved more or less for your behavior. God's love is consistent and given. One of the most compelling things I have ever seen is someone living into who they were made to be. It is a beautiful sight. And so are you.

REFLECTION QUESTIONS

- Take stock of your own inner Post-it notes. How might you remove those stickies and replace them with more helpful thoughts?

- How tired are you of being second fiddle to your most unhelpful thoughts? How brave and honest can you be in making the necessary shifts in thinking?

- What does it mean to you that you are a portable sanctuary?

- What will it look like for you to reflect on and step into your life in a more open and fresh way?

Acknowledgments

THANK YOU TO MY HUSBAND, Alan. You paved the way onto this writing journey, and I am grateful for the way you have believed in and encouraged me all along the way. I love you. These two hearts . . .

I'm grateful for my sons, Sean, Bryan, and Christopher. I love you men to pieces and I am so thankful for you. You bring me great joy.

For my dear friends Marla Christian and Stacey Green. As I made my way through the various parts of the writing process, you gently and graciously held my hopes and my fears. Thank you for walking alongside me so beautifully.

My heartfelt thanks to the women who have so graciously and vulnerably shared your stories in each of the voice chapters. This book would not be the same without their raw courage to share some of the most painful parts of your lives. Your gift to us is deeply appreciated and I am profoundly grateful. I may have used pseudonyms here, but know that I see you, and, more importantly, God sees you and is honored.

Thank you to the InterVarsity Press team for carrying me and this project along with such wisdom and grace. You make it easier to love the editing and marketing process and you helped make this book what it is. Thank you to my editors Cindy Bunch and Rachel Hastings. Thank you to Lori Neff, Krista Clayton, and Allie Noble, my marketing and publicity team; David Fassett, my book cover designer; and the rest of the IVP team!

Special thanks to Kara Yuza who helps keep my head on straight. Without your managing of all the details, I wouldn't have the brain space to lean into projects like this. Thank you for sticking with us even though you are completely overqualified. You do it all with excellence and grace. Thank you!

Thank you to our Unhurried Living board and advisory board: Tom Christian, Marla Christian, David Huseby, Cathy Huseby, Jeb Shore, Darrell Warner, Jeff Linam, Mary Linam. You believe in us, you stand with us, you pray for us. Thank you!

I want to thank the four spiritual directors who have held my stories at various times during my midlife journey and beyond. Thank you to Abbot David Geraets (1935–2012), Sister Ann Cic (1929–2017), Ellyn Cowie, and David Booram. Many of the stories contained here happened on your watch. God has graciously gifted me with your presence as you remain present to me.

Writing can only occur in moments of deep concentration and focus. Location has much to do with this kind of space. I am so grateful to Grace and Steve Cabalka for offering the use of their studio in Avila Beach, California. I am also thankful for Cathy and Dave Huseby for gifting the use of their cabin in Duck Creek, Utah. Your homes have become places of refuge for me. My body sinks into the space, and it just knows it's time to write. Thank you!

I could not be more grateful for all the women, past and present, who have chosen me as their spiritual director, coach, or mentor. Your lives and stories inspire me month by month. I see your deep desire to be formed into the image of Christ. Thank you for leaning in and allowing me to be an eyewitness to the work of the Spirit.

To the Unhurried Living extended community—donors, prayers, readers, podcast listeners, event-attenders, email recipients—your connection is priceless. May God's favor rest on you as you continue to lead from an unhurried heart.

A Refreshed Foundation

ESCAPING THE TRAP OF PUSHING, TRYING, AND ANGSTING

These ideas emerged from this prayer: *God, you have to show me a new way to live and work. My current way is no longer serving me, and I need a new level of sustainability and peace.*

This process is certainly a nice change of pace from pushing, trying, and angsting. I find each part to be a lovely reminder. Give these ideas a try and see what happens in your own life.

- *Begin* with gratitude. Transform the way you take in the world. Move from anticipation to contentment through gratitude in the moment (Psalm 107:1).

- *Consider* Jesus' invitation: *This is my body, which is for you* (1 Corinthians 11:24).

- *Let go*; release the unholy trio: Pushing. Trying. Angsting (Psalm 46:10).

- *Remember*, you already have what you need (2 Peter 1:3). You may have lost track of it. You may have forgotten it. But you have it. Life is a journey of uncovering.

- ● ***Keep in mind*** the one thing you have for sure—the care of the Trinity (2 Corinthians 13:14):
  - ● the love of God (Matthew 3:17),
  - ● the grace of Jesus (John 15), and
  - ● the fellowship of the Holy Spirit (John 14:16, 26).

In prayer we discover what we already have. You start from where you are and you deepen what you already have, and you realize you are already there. We already have everything, but we don't know it and don't experience it. Everything has been given to us in Christ. All we need is to experience what we already possess.[1]

Using Notice, Discern, Respond

RECALLING THE DINING ROOM SCENARIO from chapter two, you can use this Notice, Discern, Respond process with unhelpful thoughts so that you remain at the head of the table. It might be nice to purchase a special journal in which to do your thought work. Choose any of the seven voices and move through the questions below.

Notice

- How does this voice show up in your life?
- List a few phrases this voice typically whispers (or shouts) in your ear.

Discern

Choose one phrase you listed in the notice section and ask yourself:

- How have I come to rely on this thought?
- What is it costing me to let this thought sit at the head of the table?
- What is making it difficult for me to let go of this thought? What is keeping me stuck here?

- What is the benefit of shifting to a more helpful thought?

Further questions you can ask for greater discernment:

- Is this thought true?
- Is this just a passing thought, or would it be good to spend some time with it?
- Does this thought have a friendly tone or a critical one?
- If I said this thought out loud, would it sound encouraging or belittling?
- If I spoke this way to others, would they feel judged or helped?
- What is the fruit of this thought? Does it lead to greater love, joy, and peace—or to stress, complaining, or hopelessness?

Respond

- Based on your discernment work above, what is one new helpful thought you can begin to practice?
- What might get in the way of shifting to this new thought?
- Do you need to shift to neutral before moving to the new helpful thought?
- How can you be kind to yourself as you keep on track with your new helpful thought? Recall the *benefit* you listed in the Discern section.
- What other support might you need?
- If you notice that healing from this thought requires more assistance, what might be your next step in seeking help?

Small Group Guide

THE GUIDE BELOW IS DESIGNED for a nine-session small group or a leadership team experience. Each week, participants will read a chapter and spend time with the end-of-chapter questions in preparation for the group meeting and interaction. This guide assumes about sixty to ninety minutes spent together with the material. The amount of time will depend on how many people are in your group. You may also add on some time for prayer and additional sharing at the beginning or end of your gathering.

When in a small group with others it is good to remember that it is sacred space. It is a place of safety in which you hold one another's stories. Listen well in respect and honor. There is no need for fixing or answer giving. Being heard is an incredible gift, as is granting empathy. Share honestly and be as open as you can. And keep confidentiality to ensure everyone's privacy.

Doing your own inner work on these voices and the thoughts they represent may be difficult. Be sure to convey your feelings and give grace to yourself and one another in this process. This is important to remember throughout the process of gathering together.

SESSION ONE

Group Preparation

Before the session, read chapters one and two. Journal on the reflection questions for those chapters.

Meeting

Open by allowing time for each member to introduce themselves and share what they are hoping for over the course of reading this book. What do you hope occurs within you and your community as you share your thoughts and experiences together?

Reflect together on the questions from chapters one and two. Give time for each person to share their response to at least one of the questions from each chapter.

Close your gathering with prayers based on everyone's shared hopes.

SESSION TWO

Group Preparation

Before the session, read chapter three. Journal on the *Notice, Discern, and Respond* section for those chapters.

Meeting

Reflect together on the questions from chapter three. Give time for each person to share from their *Notice, Discern, and Respond* journal.

Close your gathering with prayers for comfort and healing for one another.

SESSION THREE

Group Preparation
Before the session, read chapter four. Journal on the *Notice, Discern, and Respond* section for those chapters.

Meeting
Reflect together on the questions from chapter four. Give time for each person to share from their *Notice, Discern, and Respond* journal.

Close your gathering with prayers for comfort and healing for one another.

SESSION FOUR

Group Preparation
Before the session, read chapter five. Journal on the *Notice, Discern, and Respond* section for those chapters.

Meeting
Reflect together on the questions from chapter five. Give time for each person to share from their *Notice, Discern, and Respond* journal.

Close your gathering with prayers for comfort and healing for one another.

SESSION FIVE

Group Preparation
Before the session, read chapter six. Journal on the *Notice, Discern, and Respond* section for those chapters.

Meeting

Reflect together on the questions from chapter six. Give time for each person to share from their *Notice, Discern, and Respond* journal.

Close your gathering with prayers for comfort and healing for one another.

SESSION SIX

Group Preparation

Before the session, read chapter seven. Journal on the *Notice, Discern, and Respond* section for those chapters.

Meeting

Reflect together on the questions from chapter seven. Give time for each person to share from their *Notice, Discern, and Respond* journal.

Close your gathering with prayers for comfort and healing for one another.

SESSION SEVEN

Group Preparation

Before the session, read chapter eight. Journal on the *Notice, Discern, and Respond* section for those chapters.

Meeting

Reflect together on the questions from chapter eight. Give time for each person to share from their *Notice, Discern, and Respond* journal.

Close your gathering with prayers for comfort and healing for one another.

SESSION EIGHT

Group Preparation
Before the session, read chapter nine. Journal on the *Notice, Discern, and Respond* section for those chapters.

Meeting
Reflect together on the questions from chapter nine. Give time for each person to share from their *Notice, Discern, and Respond* journal.

Close your gathering with prayers for comfort and healing for one another.

SESSION NINE

Group Preparation
Before the session, read chapter ten. Journal on the reflection questions for chapter ten.

Meeting
Reflect together on the questions from chapter ten. Give time for each person to share their responses to the reflection questions.

In this final meeting, make space to discuss what has been most helpful over the course of your gatherings.

What changes in your thinking or your way of life have you noticed?

What invitations did you notice?

What might be some next steps for you?

Close with prayers of gratitude and of offering your intentions to continue this transforming journey with Jesus.

Notes

1. YOU ARE MORE THAN YOUR THOUGHTS

[1]Merriam Webster defines a *trigger* as "to cause an intense and usually negative emotional reaction in someone." When I mention *trigger*, I am referring to anything that leads to an overreaction in your life. Triggers are helpful because they point directly to an area that may need healing.

[2]I first learned about the inner observer from Dr. Marie J. DiSciullo-Naples, PhD, during my training in spiritual direction with Monastery of the Risen Christ in San Luis Obispo, CA, 2005-06.

[3]Henri Nouwen, *Spiritual Direction* (New York: HarperCollins Publishers, 2006), 28-29. One of Nouwen's false identities.

[4]Thomas Keating, *Invitation to Love* (New York: Continuum Publishing, 2002), 5-7. One of Keating's programs for happiness.

[5]Nouwen, *Spiritual Direction*, 28-29.

[6]Keating, *Invitation to Love*, 5-7.

[7]Keating, *Invitation to Love*, 5-7.

[8]Nouwen, *Spiritual Direction*, 28-29.

[9]Dallas Willard, *The Divine Conspiracy* (San Francisco: HarperOne, 2009), 68.

[10]Center for Action and Contemplation, interview with James Finley and Kirsten Oates, *Turning to the Mystics: Introducing James Finley*, podcast audio, February 8, 2020, https://cac.org/podcasts/introducing-james-finley/.

[11]Alison Cook and Kimberly Miller, *Boundaries for Your Soul* (Nashville, TN: Thomas Nelson, 2018).

2. FINDING YOUR VOICE

[1]*Wonder Woman*, directed by Patty Jenkins (Burbank, CA: Warner Bros. Pictures, 2017).

[2]Deb Dana, *Befriending Your Nervous System* (Louisville, CO: Audible, 2020).

[3]Alan Fadling, *An Unhurried Leader* (Downers Grove, IL: InterVarsity Press, 2017), 137-39.

[4]This quote is attributed to Viktor Frankl, but the original published source is unknown.

[5]The idea of the inner dining table was first introduced to me by Ken Londeaux, EdD, ABMP, licensed psychologist, now retired.

3. FROM STRESSED ACHIEVER TO LIVING WITH INTENTION

[1]Pseudonyms have been used for all of the women who so graciously shared their stories.

4. FROM POSITIVE THINKER TO GROWING IN HOPE

[1]Thomas Merton, *Thoughts in Solitude* (New York: Farrar, Strauss and Cudahy, 1958, 2000), 3.

[2]Beach Boys, "Good Vibrations," *Smiley Smile*, Capitol Records, 1967.

[3]Simon Sinek, "The Best Gift You Can Give Your Team: Optimism!" Facebook post, www.facebook.com/simonsinek/, November 25, 2016.

[4]Merton, *Thoughts in Solitude*, 4-5, edited for gender inclusivity.

[5]*A Beautiful Day in the Neighborhood*, directed by Marielle Heller (Culver City, CA: TriStar Pictures, 2019).

[6]This section first appeared as the post "Hammering and Silence Do Not Go Together . . . Or Do They?" Unhurried Living, September 7, 2016, www.unhurried living.com/blog/hammering-silence.

5. FROM INNER CRITIC TO GAINING FRESH PERSPECTIVE

[1]*The Devil Wears Prada*, directed by David Frankel (Los Angeles: Fox 2000 Pictures, 2006).

6. FROM ANXIOUS CONTROLLER TO ENJOYING LIFE'S SEASONS

[1]Brené Brown, *The Power of Vulnerability* (Louisville, CO: Sounds True, 2013).

[2]Olivia (pseudonym), personal journal, March 2021. Used with permission.

[3]Bishop Todd Hunter in a sermon at Holy Trinity Church, circa 2018.

7. FROM COMPLAINING VICTIM TO WALKING IN FREEDOM

[1]If you are in an abusive or violent situation, please call the National Domestic Violence Hotline, 1-800-799-7233.

[2]Hara Estroff Marano, "Our Brain's Negative Bias: Why Our Brains Are More Highly Attuned to Negative News," *Psychology Today*, June 30, 2003, www.psychologytoday.com/us/articles/200306/our-brains-negative-bias.

[3]*The Diving Bell and the Butterfly*, directed by Julian Schnabel (Los Angeles: Pathé Distribution, Miramax Films, 2007).

[4]*Diving Bell and the Butterfly*, Schnabel.

8. FROM PASSIVE SPECTATOR TO INSPIRING THROUGH PRESENCE

[1]Macrina Weidekehr, *A Tree Full of Angels* (San Francisco: HarperOne, 2009), xiii.

9. FROM UNSETTLED HEART TO BEING AT HOME

[1]I first learned this concept from Brook Castillo, *The Life Coach School Podcast*, episode 287, September 26, 2019. I added the "grounding truth" step because I think it's good for us to have a spiritual or scriptural inspiration.

10. ENGAGING GOD'S VOICE

[1]Brené Brown shares this big idea in her book *Rising Strong* (New York: Random House, 2017).

[2]James Finley, *Merton's Palace of Nowhere* (Notre Dame, IN: Ave Maria Press, 1978), 112.

[3]Examples: Isaiah 49:15, Isaiah 66:13, Luke 13:34.

[4]Henri Nouwen, *Here and Now* (Chestnut Ridge, NY: Crossroad Publishing, 2006), 59-60.

[5]Dallas Willard, *The Great Omission* (San Francisco: HarperOne, 2014), xiv.

APPENDIX A: A REFRESHED FOUNDATION

[1]James Finley, *Merton's Palace of Nowhere* (Notre Dame, IN: Ave Maria Press, 1978), 82.

About the Author

GEM FADLING, CLC, is a founding partner of Unhurried Living, Inc., a nonprofit that trains people to rest deeper, live fuller, and lead better. She is a certified life coach and a trained spiritual director who coaches women at the intersection of spiritual leadership and soul care. Gem is the host of the *I Can Do That!* podcast and the coauthor of *What Does Your Soul Love? Eight Questions That Reveal God's Work in You.*

Also Available

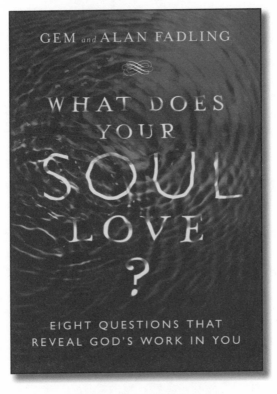

What Does Your Soul Love?
978-0-8308-4659-7

>>> unhurried**living**

Many leaders feel hurried, and hurry is costing them more than they realize. Unhurried Living, founded by Alan and Gem Fadling, provides coaching, resources, and training to help people learn to lead from fullness rather than leading on empty.

Busy is a matter of calendar. Hurry is a matter of soul.

Built on more than twenty-five years of experience at the intersection of spiritual formation and leadership development, Unhurried Living seeks to inspire Christian leaders around the world to rest deeper so they can live fuller and lead better.

Spiritual leadership is the influence that grows in the life of a leader being transformed by the power of God's Spirit. Spiritual leadership is learning to robustly practice spiritual disciplines that deepen the roots of leaders in the love of God.

Effective spiritual leaders learn to experience the depths of God's love so they know how to lead others into those same depths. Such leadership bears the fruit of transformed lives and expanded kingdom influence.

We seek to respond to questions many are asking:

Rest deeper: Why do I so often feel more drained than energized? Can I find space for my soul to breathe?

Live fuller: I have tried to fill my life with achievements, possessions, and popularity, and I feel emptier than ever. Where can I find fullness that lasts?

Lead better: How can I step off the treadmill of mere busyness and make real, meaningful progress in my life and work?

Rediscover the genius of Jesus' unhurried way of life and leadership.

Come visit us at unhurriedliving.com to discover free resources to help you

Rest Deeper. Live Fuller. Lead Better.

Web: unhurriedliving.com
Facebook: facebook.com/unhurriedliving
Instagram: UnhurriedLiving
Email: info@unhurriedliving.com

BECOMING OUR TRUE SELVES

The nautilus is one of the sea's oldest creatures. Beginning with a tight center, its remarkable growth pattern can be seen in the ever-enlarging chambers that spiral outward. The nautilus in the IVP Formatio logo symbolizes deep inward work of spiritual formation that begins rooted in our souls and then opens to the world as we experience spiritual transformation. The shell takes on a stunning pearlized appearance as it ages and forms in much the same way as the souls of those who devote themselves to spiritual practice. Formatio books draw on the ancient wisdom of the saints and the early church as well as the rich resources of Scripture, applying tradition to the needs of contemporary life and practice.

Within each of us is a longing to be in God's presence. Formatio books call us into our deepest desires and help us to become our true selves in the light of God's grace.

VISIT

ivpress.com/formatio

*to see all of the books in the
line and to sign up for the
IVP Formatio newsletter.*